Michelle Wie

Michelle Wie

THE MAKING OF A CHAMPION

Jennifer Mario

St. Martin's Griffin
New York

To Gretchen, my favorite girl golfer

www.stmartins.com

Book design by Paula Russell Szafranski

ISBN-13: 978-0-312-36289-8
ISBN-10: 0-312-36289-7

First Edition: July 2006

10 9 8 7 6 5 4 3 2 1

Contents

Contents

Preface

Everyone who loves golf has heard of Michelle Wie. The teen-aged golf phenom turned sixteen years old in October of 2005, then turned professional, signing endorsements that made her an instant millionaire before she'd even gotten her driver's license.

Crowds love her. Sponsors love her. TV networks love her—tournaments that a year ago received very little coverage become highly rated events when Michelle joins the field. Case in point: The 2005 John Deere Classic tournament's gross revenue went up 40 percent and TV ratings were up 54 percent over last year (to more than 2 million viewers) with Michelle in the field.

According to ABC golf analyst Judy Rankin, "Michelle is one of the four or five most interesting players in golf today. She's right there with Tiger Woods, Ernie Els, Vijay Singh, and Annika Sorenstam." LPGA Tour commissioner Carolyn Bivens described Michelle as "a young woman with phenomenal talent who brings the promise of incredible performance and a marketability that will draw fans of all ages from all corners of the world into the sport of golf like never before."

As *Fortune* magazine declared simply in their cover article on Wie, "Michelle sells."

So what drives this popularity? What is it about a sixteen-year-old Korean-American girl from Honolulu that causes such a furor? Well, it just might be her talent. A golfer since the age of four, she's been playing with and beating adults almost all of her short life. Her father, BJ, a university professor, and mother, Bo, a Realtor, are both avid golfers. BJ, a 2-handicap player, and Bo, a Korean women's amateur champion, taught Michelle golf at an early age. By age eight, she could beat both of them.

At a willowy six feet tall, she stands, literally, head and shoulders above the rest. She can drive the ball more than 300 yards and has competed against the best in the world. She hasn't missed an LPGA cut since she turned fourteen. She played in only seven LPGA events in 2005 as an amateur, yet the money she would have earned topped $640,000—second in average earnings to only one player, Annika Sorenstam. Also in 2005, Michelle placed in the top three in half of her LPGA tournaments.

Her career reads like a world records entry: youngest player to qualify in a USGA amateur championship event (age ten); youngest winner of Hawaii State Women's Golf Association Stroke-Play Championship (age eleven); youngest player to qualify for an LPGA tournament by Monday qualifying (age twelve); youngest player to make an LPGA cut (age thirteen, at the Kraft Nabisco Championship, a major); youngest player to win the U.S. Women's Amateur Public Links Championship (age thirteen). The list goes on and on.

But it's not just her LPGA appearances that have garnered

all this attention. Because Michelle doesn't limit herself to the LPGA. Instead, she's set a goal for herself that no woman has ever achieved: to play against men, to join the PGA Tour.

And she's not wasting any time; she's already played in four PGA Tour events and done admirably well. Not even Tiger Woods performed as well in his first PGA Tour events as Michelle Wie did. In her first foray into the PGA Tour, the 2004 Sony Open, she missed the cut by only one stroke. She was fourteen. In Tiger's first PGA Tour event, he was sixteen, and missed the cut by six.

But with success and a place in the spotlight has come something else: criticism. Michelle hasn't taken the traditional path that most golfers have traveled—that of playing first in junior events, then in amateur tournaments, then, finally, and only after qualifying, professional events. This is how you learn to win, critics say. Playing against people she can't possibly beat is bad for her and bad for the game.

The critics do have a point: Whereas Tiger Woods played (and won) every junior and amateur event there is to play, Michelle Wie has leapfrogged right over them, skipping "dues paying" altogether in order to compete at the highest level possible. But Michelle isn't bothered by critics. Her response? "I'm not looking for 100 percent support. I know there are going to be people against me. I'm not going to stop just for them."

At such a young age, she's become both an icon and a pioneer. In her first meeting with her sports psychologist, Dr. Jim Loehr, she confided to him that she was on a mission: to communicate to women that there are no boundaries. In golf, this is definitely thinking outside the box. Now, at sixteen, just a junior in high school, she's become the youngest, wealthiest professional female golfer in the world.

Her former coach Casey Nakama credits her for an increased interest in golf among young girls. "In the past six months, in the past year, we have an increased enrollment in girls," he says. "When you enter our program, you have to go through a series of classes, and it's always been about 20 percent, 30 percent girls. But this year it's gone up to 50 percent and I've had a class with more girls than boys, I had about 80 percent girls—fifteen girls, three boys, something like that. I think some of the girls now, they want to try. Golf is a little bit more cool to play." It's not just new fans Michelle is creating, it's new golfers.

As a golf writer, I was curious about her when I began this project. Now, as a mother, I hold her up as a role model for my children. I watch her on television with my daughter; I describe her talent and hard work to my sons. But she's not just a model for children; adults can learn a thing or two from her as well. She works hard. She faces her opponents without fear. She keeps her poise. She seems to have no concept of either limitations or gender barriers. All while getting her homework finished before 9:00 P.M.

Why write a biography of Michelle Wie? Michelle Wie's life, values, work ethic, and driving ambition are enough to inspire not just teens, not just golfers, but everyone. "Dream big and I will reach the sky; dream small and my feet will never get off the ground," she wrote in a letter to the Associated Press. As her coach David Leadbetter has said, "We don't know what she's capable of; she might change the game as we know it."

Michelle Wie

Introduction

The ball fell into the cup with a decisive rattle, eliciting a roar from the crowd so loud it could be heard from several holes away. Heads turned toward the sixteenth green, as fans wondered aloud what had happened to make the crowd react so wildly. Surely someone had just made a birdie, or maybe even an eagle. Could it have been Ernie Els, the defending champion and now the tournament leader?

The crowd gathered around the sixteenth hole there at Waialae Country Club in Honolulu, Hawaii, was packed five and six deep, so it was hard to catch a glimpse of the tall golfer striding briskly on to the next hole. But then, for just a moment, the crowd parted, and there she was.

It was Michelle Wie, the most unlikely of players, who had made that birdie. She'd started the hole with a 311-yard drive, her longest drive of the day, then followed it up with a pitching wedge that landed just 15 feet away from the flag. She studied the hole from all angles, conferred with her caddie, then, with a smooth, even stroke, sank the putt.

No one thought Michelle would be making birdies today—except maybe Michelle. Why? Because at fourteen, she was the youngest golfer ever to play a PGA Tour event. Not only that, she was a girl. That day was Friday, January 16, 2004, and the setting was the 2004 Sony Open.

The golf season starts right here, in Honolulu, Hawaii, each year, with the first full-field event, the Sony Open. This year was no different, except for the fact that this time, a fourteen-year-old girl would be joining the 143 PGA Tour players.

Michelle had just two holes left to play in her second round before everyone's question would be answered: Would she make the cut? Could a fourteen-year-old girl be the first woman to make a cut in a PGA Tour event since Mildred "Babe" Didrikson Zaharias did it in 1945 at the Los Angeles Open? To pull it off, Michelle would need to go two under in those last two holes.

Michelle strode on to hole 17, a par 3. She wound up, pulled her club back with her usual fluid motion, and swung, but the ball shot left, bouncing off the grandstands and landing in the rough. Not about to give up, she took out a wedge, pitched to just a few feet from the flag, and saved her par.

Would it be enough? She still had a chance, but now she would need an eagle on the final hole. The crowds around Michelle had grown even larger, nearly five thousand large, larger than the ones surrounding some of the tournament's biggest names, such as Vijay Singh and Davis Love III. Everyone wanted to watch this piece of history being made.

The crowd made way for her as she moved on to number 18. This would be the deciding moment. As the sun began to set, Michelle carefully teed up her ball, ready to do battle with this 551-yard par 5. Boom! She split the fairway with a 299-yard drive, leaving 252 yards to the hole, a shot she could place on the green without too much difficulty. One more shot to the green, plus a single putt, would give her the eagle she needed. She pulled out her 5 wood.

But her shot didn't quite make it. It landed and rolled, coming to rest a few feet short of the green. With the crowd holding its collective breath, she made her chip shot. It rolled right toward the flag. For a second it looked like it might just go in the hole, but it kept rolling, snaking just a few feet past. Michelle made the birdie putt, but it wasn't enough. Her chances at an eagle were over, and with it her chance of making the cut.

As she sat in the scorer's tent after her round, she realized how close she had come. She had missed the cut by *one stroke.* Her dream to make the cut in a PGA Tour event would have to wait, because her two rounds at even par weren't quite good enough.

But with all that disappointment, Michelle had plenty of reasons to be proud. She had set a record that day: Not only was she the youngest person ever to play in a Tour event, but she also made the lowest score ever shot by a woman playing against men, a 68.

Besides which, she could have been back at school, finishing up geometry and biology exams the way her classmates were that very day. Instead she was out on the golf course playing with some of her golf heroes, the best golfers in the world, and setting new records.

Before the tournament began, Michelle had thought it out. "It's a lot different from other tournaments because it's the

Sony Open," she said in an interview with the press. "It's a men's PGA event. But I think I'm just going to go in with the same attitude that I go into the LPGA tournaments and the amateur tournaments. It's just that I'm playing against different people."

Michelle was no stranger to golf tournaments. She'd been playing in them her whole life, since she first started playing the game at age four. In her home state of Hawaii, she'd won just about every tournament there was to win, from the Jennie K. Wilson Invitational, the most prestigious women's amateur tournament in the state, to the Women's Division of the Hawaii State Open. Each time she played against opponents two, three, and sometimes even four times her age, and beat them.

Just a year earlier she had won the U.S. Women's Amateur Public Links Championship, a tournament that brings together many of America's best amateur female golfers.

But the Sony Open was special: It was her introduction to the PGA Tour, and the start of a dream. Michelle had always wanted to play against the best golfers in the world, both male and female, and this was the first time she'd had the chance. Earlier that week, she'd gotten to play a practice round with Ernie Els, the defending champion of the tournament and its eventual winner.

Els had plenty of nice things to say about Michelle. He could have been annoyed at being saddled with a teenaged girl as a playing partner—but in fact, he was the one who had arranged it. He told the press afterward how much he'd enjoyed his round with her, saying, "We had a beautiful day. It was nice watching Michelle swing the club. She's a true phenomenon and she's a great, great person and we had a fun morning."

Introduction

Who is this girl, the one who likes to watch Johnny Depp movies and listens to Coldplay, the one who loves big, huggable dogs and can drive a golf ball more than 300 yards at will—the girl who's played with CEOs and presidents? In some ways she's just an ordinary girl, and in other ways she's bigger than life.

Michelle Wie is a big talent, with big dreams to match. But her story doesn't begin at the 2004 Sony Open. It goes back much further, to a day ten years prior. That day in 1994, her parents took Michelle out to a baseball field, put a golf club in Michelle's tiny four-year-old hands, and watched as she swung for the fences.

1

The Early Years

I like to be the first to do anything.
I like to be the best.

At just sixteen years old, Michelle Sung Wie has made quite a name for herself in the golf world. She's been playing with professionals since she was twelve and has become not just an icon but also a role model for kids and adults alike.

But golf wasn't always the only sport in Michelle's life. When she was little, her parents tried to expose her to as many activities as possible. She gave them all a chance: baseball, soccer, tennis, and of course golf. But it wasn't long before it became clear that other sports weren't for her—they involved way too much running, which Michelle can't stand.

Maybe golf is in her genes. Her father, BJ (short for Byung Wook), is an avid golfer and a 2-handicap player (very good, in other words—see the sidebar on page 20). And her mother, Hyun Kyong (nicknamed Bo), was an amateur champion back in South Korea, where both Michelle's parents are from.

Bo loved golf so much that she taught her husband to play.

He was hooked immediately. So it seemed only natural that when Michelle was born she would love it, too—and she did. They started, when she was four years old, by having her hit some balls at a nearby baseball field. After she knocked a few right out of the park, they brought her to the range instead. Michelle took to golf right away. She would follow her parents to the course and hit balls with them for hours.

Even now her parents stay with her when she practices; they sit next to her as she hits bucket after bucket of balls, rolling her balls back to her as she putts. An only child, Michelle always got plenty of attention from her parents.

Michelle showed signs of precociousness in many areas, not just golf. According to her parents, she began walking at just nine months and also showed an early talent for academics. "We asked her to solve algebraic questions when she was about ten," BJ told John Hopkins of the London *Times*. "She is a fast reader. She was really good at reading, English, mathematics, at a young age, but we spent more energy at golf. She started practicing her autograph at a very young age. She was reading and recognizing letters at age one."

This shouldn't come as too much of a surprise, considering her father has a Ph.D. (in city and regional planning) from the Ivy League's University of Pennsylvania. He works as a professor in the School of Travel Industry Management at the University of Hawaii at Manoa, although he has taken some time off to travel with Michelle. Michelle's uncle Bong Wie is a professor of mechanical and aerospace engineering at Arizona State, and her grandfather Sang-Kyu Wie retired from a career as professor of aeronautics at Seoul National University (Korea's equivalent of Harvard—its most prestigious university). It's not a stretch to say that intelligence runs in the Wie family.

If not for golf, Michelle might be pursuing a career in academics as well. Even as a child, she declared that her goal was to someday be a professor, like her father, uncle, and grandfather. Stanford was, and still is, her school of choice. For one thing, it's known for its top golf team. For another, she has a family connection to the school, since Stanford is where her uncle received his doctorate and her grandfather taught as a visiting professor. And of course, it doesn't hurt that her golf hero, Tiger Woods, attended Stanford. Though turning pro means she won't be able to play on Stanford's golf team, she can still arrange to study there, even while playing professional tournaments.

Michelle's mother, Bo, is no slouch herself. She received her Realtor's license and works as a successful real estate agent in Honolulu. Both parents were born in Seoul (the capital of South Korea) but met and married in Los Angeles in 1987 before making their way to Honolulu two years later. Michelle was born later that same year, on October 11, 1989.

BJ and Bo played in a local league at the Olomana Golf Links, a club near their home in Honolulu, just off the Kalanianaole Highway. Michelle would come along just to follow them, but it wasn't long before her parents were tagging along after her.

She could hit a ball 100 yards not long after picking up clubs for the first time—she always swung as hard as possible. The first time Michelle played a full 18-hole round, at age seven, she scored an 86—keep in mind there are plenty of adults who play golf for years and never score that well. At age nine, she broke par—an amazing accomplishment many adults never achieve (see the following sidebar).

The Shortest Golf Lesson You'll Ever Take

Here's a quick lesson on the way golf is played, in case you're not familiar with the game. A golf course has eighteen holes, and the object of the game is to complete each hole in as few strokes as possible. "Par" is the term given to the number of strokes a hole is ideally played in. A good player will complete a "par-4" hole in four strokes. It should take two hits to reach the green, then two putts to get the ball into the hole. A "bogey" is one shot over par—making a five on a par-4 hole or a four on a par 3. A double bogey is two shots over par, a triple bogey is three shots over par, and so on. Golf holes are always par 3, 4, or 5.

A "birdie," however, is one shot *under* par. That's what good players aim for, because birdies keep your score low and win matches. Occasionally a player will even make an "eagle." That means they scored two shots under par—a hole in one on a par 3, for example, or a three on a par 5. Eagles are pretty rare, and quite a thrill. Breaking par—shooting an entire round of golf under par—is very difficult. Only the very best golfers break par consistently.

It wasn't just talent Michelle inherited from her parents; she acquired a serious work ethic as well. Even as a child, she would practice hitting balls for hours every day—three or four hours after school, then seven or eight hours on weekends. Her parents would come along, and her father would check her swing against photos of Tiger Woods that he kept in his wallet. By age eight, she could beat both of her parents.

Catch a Tiger by the Toe

For years, Michelle claimed Tiger Woods as her golf hero. He was (and still is) one of the best golfers in the world, perhaps even the best that's ever been—a goal that Michelle herself aspires to. It began when she was seven years old and her father had her watch the 1997 Masters. Tiger blew the field away by twelve shots. BJ fostered Michelle's interest in Tiger by papering her room with photos of Tiger and using Tiger's swing to guide Michelle's.

Michelle can't bring herself to take those old posters of Tiger down. "I have some actors that I like that I want to put up," she laughed during a press conference at one point. "But, no. It's like seven years old and I can't take it off. I kind of want to take it off, but I kind of don't." Michelle even joked with *Golf Today* that BJ "doesn't have a picture of me in his wallet, but he has two pictures of Tiger."

It's appropriate that Michelle wants to follow in Tiger's footsteps because, like her, he's broken many of golf's records: At age fifteen, he was the youngest to win the U.S. Junior Amateur; at age eighteen, he became the youngest to win the U.S. Amateur; at age twenty-one, he became the youngest-ever Masters champion; and at age twenty-five, he was the youngest-ever career Grand Slam winner.

Tiger, like Michelle, has also been credited with breaking golf barriers. For Tiger, it was the race barrier—he was the first golfer of color to win a major. Tiger is considered African-American by most, although he is actually a blend of several races—his father is part African-American, part American Indian, and part Chinese. His mother is half-Thai, one-quarter Chinese, and one-quarter Caucasian. For Michelle, it's the gender barrier—she plays in tournaments traditionally reserved for men and has the goal of one day joining the PGA Tour.

Tiger's talent was recognized even earlier than Michelle's was—when he was just two years old, he appeared on *The Mike Douglas Show* for a putting contest against Bob Hope.

When the BBC (British Broadcasting Company) asked Michelle why she likes Tiger, she answered, "Tiger has broken down barriers and it would be great if I could help women to compete against men. . . . I've met Tiger once and it was really neat. Both him, Ernie Els, and Annika Sorenstam are role models to me."

FINDING A COACH

When they began losing to their eight-year-old regularly, BJ and Bo realized that it was time to get Michelle some professional instruction. Recognizing that their child had real potential in competitive golf, they sought out an instructor who could teach Michelle not just how to swing a club properly but also how to compete. They wanted an instructor with playing experience, someone who had won in tournament situations.

The natural first place to look was the Olomana Golf Links in Honolulu, where they spent most of their leisure time. The instructor they chose was Casey Nakama.

Casey Nakama runs a golf school for juniors at Olomana, the Casey Nakama Golf Development Center. At the time, Nakama had built a reputation for himself as a strong competitor, having played professionally on the Asia Golf Circuit and having won many local tournaments, including the JAL Rainbow Open, the Hawaii State Open, the Maui Open (twice), the Makaha Open, the Hilo Open, the Waikoloa Open, and the Mid-Pacific Open.

To the Wies, it was critical that Michelle's coach would have real-life competition experience. Says Nakama, "Mr. Wie wanted a player-teacher to help Michelle, rather than just a teacher. At that time I was still competing in tournaments here, and I was still in contention in most of the tournaments here, so they chose me based on my reputation as a player. The feeling of being in contention, the feeling of having to make a cut, that is a feeling only players understand. A teacher who's never been in that situation could never tell a player what it feels like. So that's one thing I could pass on to them because I've been in a lot of those situations, trying to make cuts, trying to win golf tournaments."

You might wonder if Michelle stood out right away, if her talent was immediately obvious to her first coach. The answer is no. What impressed him about her wasn't her talent but her height: "She was taller than most of the girls that we had. But she wasn't doing anything out of the ordinary; she wasn't one of the better players. It's just that she was a little bit stronger than most of the girls." At age nine, Michelle already stood 5' 7", and was still growing.

By the end of her time with Nakama, that had changed; Michelle would soon be winning tournaments around the entire state of Hawaii.

But where did she start? What were her first lessons like? According to Nakama, they started with the basics. He could see that her initial training with her parents had left her with a sound swing, but a few adjustments were in order. "The first few sessions we had were in fixing up some mechanical, some basic fundamental stuff with her pitching motion," he recalls.

"Since she was taller for her age, I always felt that she would hit shorter clubs than most of the other girls. So we worked on her wedges right away. We worked on her grip a little bit, put it in a more neutral position. We just fixed up the pitching motion basically, and we fixed up her short game swing."

What Michelle may have initially lacked in skill she made up for with her work ethic. While most of the kids in Nakama's program were there just to have fun, Michelle showed right away that she could put in serious effort. After her weekly lesson, Michelle would spend hours perfecting her new skill.

"Even at ten years old, she didn't mind practicing every day. For whatever reason that separates her from other players, she was just determined to do whatever we were working on. We would make a swing adjustment, and she would work on it, and she would come back in three or four days and say, 'I think I got it, Casey.' She was just determined in that way. That work ethic that she had, it separates her from a lot of the other players."

With most of his students, Nakama had to remind them to practice the skills they learn during lessons. Not so with Michelle: "She was self-motivated and she did it on her own. Whatever we worked on for that week, she would be here for the next three, four days in a row, working on it. I didn't have to tell her how much time to practice because she practiced more than enough."

The club encouraged her to practice as much as she wanted, allowing her free use of the range. Her mother would pick her up from school and they would head straight to the golf course, with Michelle finishing her homework in the back-

A Note on Golf Clubs

Maybe you've noticed that there are several types of golf clubs. Some golf clubs have thin, flat clubheads; these are called *irons*. The angle of the clubhead determines the distance the ball will travel. Players use irons for shorter shots that need to be very accurate. Some clubheads are large and rounded; these are called *woods* (although they're not actually made out of wood anymore; these days they're made out of very high-tech metals). Woods are used for hitting longer distances but are somewhat harder to control.

So what did Nakama mean when he said Michelle "would hit shorter clubs than most of the other girls"?

Irons come in a spectrum of lengths and loft angles. The "short" clubs are the sand and pitching wedges and the 9 iron. "Long" clubs are the 2, 3, and 4 irons. They're long in the shaft, and also they hit the ball farther. "Midlength" clubs are everything in between—5, 6, 7, and 8 irons. Short clubs are easier to hit and more accurate than long clubs, but the ball does not travel as far.

When Nakama said that Michelle would hit shorter clubs than the other girls, what he meant was that because she was so much taller and stronger than her peers, she could hit a short iron on shots that would require other players to use a long club. She could therefore be more accurate and hit fewer errant shots than her opponents.

seat. Luckily for her, homework never took very long. "They tell me I'm a really fast learner," she told Jeff Merron of ESPN at one point. "Other people, they take like two hours to do their homework. I finish in like fifteen minutes. I don't know how I do that."

And when she was out of school for the summer, she would take advantage of all those extra practice hours, showing up at the course by 9:30 A.M. and playing until dark.

Michelle's willingness to put in the long hours may have had something to do with her upbringing. She was, after all, raised by two Korean parents, and they raised her with Korean values—specifically, they taught her that, first, success comes only with very hard work and, second, education is paramount.

Take a look at the life of someone Michelle's age living in Korea. A typical high-schooler's schedule goes something like this: school from 7:30 A.M. until 4:00 P.M. An after-school tutoring program until 7:00 or 8:00 P.M. Dinner and chores, then late nights completing homework or practicing a musical instrument. Caught up on all your homework? Then it's time to read ahead, study a foreign language, or practice for college entrance exams. In the United States, students begin learning calculus in college. In Korea, calculus is standard for tenth-graders. If a child is particularly gifted in a sport or music, they spend twenty or more hours a week perfecting their skills. Free time for students is not just rare; it's unheard of.

It's hard for Americans to imagine subjecting their children to that lifestyle of constant work, but for Korean parents there's nothing unusual about it. They feel lowering their expectations would be a disservice to their children, because ultimately, a strong work ethic breeds success. To Koreans, allowing their

What's the Best Way to Get Started in Golf?

Lessons, lessons, lessons. Michelle was fortunate to have a champion golfer in the family to get her started—her mother. Not everyone can be so lucky. Whatever your age—if you're a child, a teen, or an adult—the best advice is to start with lessons. Private lessons are the best, at least at the beginning. Find a qualified USGA-certified teaching instructor in your area who can teach the basics, then put in the practice hours.

You don't have to practice twenty hours a week or more like Michelle in order to learn the game. Casey Nakama, who taught Michelle from when she was almost ten until after she turned thirteen, recommends a more moderate approach for kids anyway. "They've got to get in a program that teaches them the rules correctly, and they've got to have fun playing," he says. "The program has to let the kids have fun. If it gets to be a serious program at eight, nine years old, that's crazy. At the beginning, my suggestion is just to keep it fun."

Gary Gilchrist, who coached Michelle at the David Leadbetter Golf Academy from when she was twelve until she turned fifteen and now runs the junior golf program at the International Junior Golf Academy in Hilton Head Island, South Carolina, offers this advice: "My suggestion is to find somebody to be the coach and let the parents be the parents. Today too many parents are trying to be both the coaches and the parents."

Gilchrist also offers Tiger Woods's family as a model. "If you want to learn from the best, buy Tiger Woods's three DVDs and watch how Earl Woods brought up Tiger. He would take him for lessons and let the coach teach. He would be there to support and encourage him. And don't compare your kids against other kids. You can learn a lot from other kids who are better, but comparing them to other kids is just going to break them down."

The price of lessons varies, of course, from around twenty dollars an hour for group lessons, to over one hundred dollars an hour for private, one-on-one instruction. Junior golf camps, which usually start accepting children at age seven or eight, can also be a great way to introduce kids to the sport and will teach kids the fundamentals of the swing as well as the rules of golf. Check with your local public course; many run junior camps during the summer months.

children freedom over their schedule would be irresponsible, a guaranteed path to failure. This is the upbringing that Michelle's parents had in Korea, and the one they passed along to her.

But before you start thinking that Michelle lives a deprived life, keep in mind that living in the United States—particularly in laid-back Hawaii—Michelle enjoys far more freedoms than her Korean school-age counterparts. She spends time with her friends and enjoys shopping and hobbies like drawing and designing earrings. In her interests, she's all-American. But her work ethic is as Korean as can be. The good news is, Michelle thrives on this schedule and wouldn't change a thing.

TRAINING WITH CASEY NAKAMA

Nakama's program emphasizes not just swing training but on-course experience as well. His students generally spend some time in individual lessons and also learn the rules of the game, etiquette, club selection, course management, and strategy by playing on the course itself.

Nakama kept things interesting for Michelle by having her try a variety of drills and exercises. While many instructors simply have their charges pound bucket after bucket of balls on the range, his lessons focused on actual match situations. To get her accustomed to unusual lies, he had her practice hitting balls out from behind trees and introduced complex shots, including hooks, fades, and draws.

"As a player sometimes we run into problems and you've got to be able to do certain things, so that was this thing that we did, hit running 5 irons and 7 irons, trying to get her ready for some trouble shots," he says. She loved the games he would design for her. "It's important to keep things fun," Nakama says.

Michelle had what golf instructors dream of—coachability—and Nakama appreciated this. "When we worked on something, in the following week I would see her and I would know that the change would already be made," he says.

All that work paid off. At age ten, Michelle shot an 8-under-par 64 at Olomana, a score that still ranks as her personal best. Her mother might have credited something else as well. Every day, she created a concoction for Michelle using ginseng, some herbs, and juices from goat and snake—an old Korean recipe that has supposed mental and strength benefits. Not surpris-

What Does It Mean to Have a Handicap?

You may have heard people discussing their "handicaps" and wondered what it's all about. In golf, a handicap is a way to keep competition level, so that not-so-good golfers can compete against really good golfers and still have a chance to win. A high handicap, say 15 or higher, means that you're given more strokes—so if you score a 90, your score is adjusted by fifteen strokes, to a 75. A lower handicap, say in the single digits, means that you're given fewer strokes. If a 5-handicap player shoots a 90, his or her score would be adjusted to an 85. So even though the two players shot the exact same score, the higher-handicap player would win the match after the scores were adjusted.

The formula for determining a golfer's handicap is very complex, but it's like a golf score: Lower is better. And to have no handicap is to be a "scratch player," meaning you receive no strokes at all—you can't get much better than that, unless you're a professional.

Annika Sorenstam once related a story about her first time talking to Michelle Wie. When they met, Michelle was just twelve years old. "What's your handicap?" asked Sorenstam. "I don't have one," replied Michelle. Annika was amazed, since she herself had been seventeen before she became a scratch player.

ingly, Michelle wasn't a fan, grimacing with every swallow, but she drank it anyway. Consider it an indication of her commitment to improving.

Yet even with her scores dropping and her practice time expanding, Michelle was still just a kid. "She still was the same, when she was here—she was just a teenager," says Nakama. "That was the amazing thing; she would be in the office watching TV, watching cartoons, and she would be a typical kid. But then when she stepped outside and started playing golf, her concentration level would change." On the course Michelle became as serious as any elite athlete. But off the course she was a normal child, enjoying hanging out at the mall and watching television (anything from *Tom and Jerry* to *American Idol*) and silly movies (she once called *Dumb & Dumber* her "ultimate favorite").

FAST FACTS

Michelle's favorite movie:
Dumb & Dumber

Michelle's best golf round:
a 64 at Olomana Golf Links

Michelle's first instructor:
Casey Nakama

"I can really separate my own life and golf," she said once during a Q & A with the LPGA. "It's not really hard to take me away from golf. I just love it so much that I always come back. But I love vacations, I love shopping, going out with my friends. I don't know, I'm not really . . . an all-golf kind of person. I have my own life, too."

Michelle's First Accomplishments

▶ Age 4: Took her first golf swing.

▶ Age 7: Played her first full round of golf; shot an 86.

▶ Age 8: Could beat both of her parents.

▶ Age 9: Began private lessons with Casey Nakama at the Olomana Golf Links.

▶ Age 9: Broke par for the first time.

2

Raising the Bar

People always ask why I do what I
do and why not just follow the
conventional path. My answer is
very simple. I always wanted to
push myself to the limit.

Although Michelle has said that she loved golf from the first time she picked up a club, her old coach, Casey Nakama, thinks otherwise. "When we first got started, I don't think she really loved golf; I think she liked it. But as she got better and she saw that she had an advantage playing this game, because of her strength, then she started to like the game a little bit more because she could really dominate. Of course with anything, if you're the best then you're going to enjoy it a little bit more. Competing made her even more driven. Even at eleven years old, she got really intense."

That competitive streak has stood Michelle in good stead. The legendary Babe Didrikson Zaharias (see the following sidebar) would reportedly enter locker rooms before a tournament and call out, "Okay, ladies, who's playing for second?"

Tell Me More About Babe Didrikson Zaharias

Michelle follows in the footsteps of some golfing greats—Annika Sorenstam and Mildred "Babe" Didrikson Zaharias, to name just two. When it comes to women's golf, Babe was the ultimate pioneer.

Born in 1911, Babe was an athlete of the highest caliber. In a time when few women played sports, Babe played all of them. She started with basketball, then moved on to track and field, making it all the way to the 1932 Olympics, where she won two gold medals in javelin and 80-meter hurdles and one silver medal in the high jump. She would have entered even more events, but women were only allowed to enter three at that time. She took up golf relatively late in life, at age twenty-four, but proceeded to dominate, winning thirty-five tournaments in her twenty-year career, including five majors. To groove her swing, she would hit over one thousand balls a day, staying on the range for ten hours at a time.

We can thank Babe for many things, from blazing a trail for women in sports to co-founding the LPGA. She was one of thirteen ladies who started the LPGA in 1950, mainly so they would have more opportunities to play the game.

Like Michelle, Babe was the child of immigrants—her parents moved to Texas from their home country of Norway. Michelle is fully aware of Babe's contributions to golf—most particularly the fact that she made the cut on the PGA Tour in 1945. "She was amazing beyond words," Michelle told the press after reading Babe's autobiography, *This Life I've Led*. "I read her book and I think she is awesome. What she did—

Olympics, playing in the men's events. Winning a lot of women's events. She had such a great combination of the stuff she did by playing men's events and women's events. I think she is awesome."

Babe died of cancer in 1956, at the age of forty-five. Now, fifty years after her death, she can still stake a claim as the greatest all-around female athlete of all time.

Michelle has many things in common with Babe, including a killer instinct. At just twelve years old, Michelle told *The Honolulu Advertiser,* "Some players, you can just sort of tell when you're getting to them. It's like they die, die, die-die-die, and then, you know . . . they die." Even then, there was nothing Michelle liked better than to get the best of her opponents.

Of course, like many kids, Michelle was motivated by something else as well: pocket money. For every par she made on the course, her parents gave her a quarter. Over time, the amount grew, all the way up to five dollars for each birdie.

So she may not have been a superstar right out of the gate, but Michelle did show talent and a strong work ethic. And, importantly, the drive to win. Nakama placed her in many of the area's junior competitions, where she excelled.

She joined Oahu's Junior Golf Association, where she handily won five of the seven tournaments she entered her first year. Then, under Nakama's tutelage, Michelle attempted to qualify for the Women's Amateur Public Links Championship—a national tournament—at ten years, nine months, and twenty-four days old—and made it, becoming the youngest player ever to do so.

Nakama points to that tournament as Michelle's turning

point: "After she qualified for the Women's Public Links that first year, she was ten years old, she made history being the youngest player to qualify for the Women's Public Links. When she came back, that's when her motivation grew. At that point she wanted to practice more and play more in those big tournaments."

According to Nakama, that's when Michelle really fell in love with golf: when she learned she could compete against adults.

And that's exactly what she did. At age eleven, Wie won the Hawaii State Women's Golf Association Stroke Play Championship, then received an age waiver to play in the prestigious Jennie K. Wilson Invitational, a tournament for amateur women. The waiver paid off, because she ended up winning the tournament wire-to-wire (meaning she led the entire time), beating Bobbi Kokx, the thirty-nine-year-old defending champion, by nine strokes.

As Kokx, a former university golf coach, told *The Honolulu Advertiser,* "There are some good fourteen-year-olds, and sixteen- and seventeen-year-olds, but not many eleven-year-olds who have that physique and that complete package. It's incredible to watch her play. . . . I still joke that I think I could've taken her when she was nine. If you're going to come in second to someone, why not Michelle Wie?"

Kokx's comments reflect not just Michelle's wire-to-wire win but also the growing amount of attention she was beginning to receive. The Hawaiian golf community is not terribly large, and Michelle's name began popping up in newspapers regularly.

That fall, Jay Leno's people gave the Wies a call, inviting Michelle to appear on the show. But Michelle's parents weren't interested; it was the beginning of a new school year—sixth grade—and BJ and Bo wanted Michelle to get serious about school. That kind of publicity would have distracted her too much and would have to wait for a later date.

It wasn't just a new school year Michelle was starting—it was a new school altogether. She was leaving Star of the Sea Elementary—the private Catholic school she had attended since preschool—and moving on to the Punahou School, Honolulu's most prestigious private institution (see the following sidebar).

The Punahou School

Attending the Punahou (pronounced "poo-na-hoe") School is no small deal. Founded in 1841 by early missionaries to Hawaii, the school now has 3,750 students, and is recognized as one of the finest private schools in the country. Michelle isn't the only famous alum. Illinois senator Barack Obama was a member of the class of 1979, and America Online co-founder Steve Case, the man who brought Instant Messaging to the world, graduated in 1976.

Punahou's curriculum is rigorous, and tuition is steep—$13,775 a year in 2006. But 97 to 99 percent of its graduates go on to college, and the average SAT score is 1307—which is why the Wies chose it for their daughter. They wanted Michelle to excel not just at golf but at academics as well. The value of a good education is a cornerstone of Korean culture, and for Michelle, as the child of a university professor, education came first.

The focus on education has paid off, says Laurel Bowers Husain, director of communications at Punahou: "Education is really a priority in her family. And she demonstrates it in her own work. One thing that I've heard said is that some of the things that make her a great golfer make her a great student. Her teachers consistently say that she always comes to school prepared, she's always ready to roll. And I think in that respect she's a strong student, because she really focuses on her studies and puts the effort into it."

Is it possible that a young celebrity like Michelle can have a normal school experience? Husain says yes. "[Her classmates] just treat her like everybody else. She's their friend; she's a student; she has to take tests; they just read about her in the paper, too. And I think because of who she is, the friendships that she has here, they treat her very normally. Within this school, it's a very normal life. She giggles like other kids do; she forgets her ID card; it's very normal for her here."

Michelle's golf tournaments require travel, occasionally during the school year. But she doesn't get to skip out on her schoolwork. Her teachers accommodate Michelle's tournaments, but she still has to complete coursework ahead of time or take it with her in order to keep up with her class.

It wasn't long before Michelle's parents began placing her in tournaments not just against adults but against adult *men*. "For lack of competition [in Hawaii], Mr. Wie started to enter her in some men's events," says Nakama. The motivation wasn't to go out and beat the men, but simply to seek out a higher level of competition. The lessons she would learn from strong adult players—particularly men—taught her more than what she would learn by continuing to play in junior events.

In fact, Michelle already had some experience "playing with the boys." During recess at school, she joined the boys on the basketball court. And back in the days before she had settled on golf, she played on the school's baseball team—the boys' baseball team. She never saw her gender as a barrier, even as a small child. "Ever since I was very young, I wanted to play with the guys," she told reporters recently. "I had a choice of playing softball (with girls) or baseball (with boys). I played baseball. I think that's just my characteristic."

Her first experience playing golf against men was at the ninety-third Manoa Cup Hawaii State Amateur Match-Play Championship, a men's tournament in Honolulu. There she made history once again by becoming not just the youngest player but also the first woman to qualify. She qualified again the following year, in 2002, winning her first match. Her second match went to extra holes, but she ended up losing to thirty-six-year-old Del-Marc Fujita, one of Hawaii's best amateurs, by one stroke.

Fujita later told *Golf for Women* magazine that he had been lucky to pull out that victory: "I was very lucky to win. She had me down three strokes after nine holes. I mean, her shot trajectory and strength are amazing. I literally had to force myself to stop watching her swing. I looked at the sky instead. She was driving as far as I was on most holes; she was already, like, six inches taller than me; and pretty soon I was thinking, 'What advantage do I really have here?'"

THOUGH PROUD OF her successes, her coach did have some concern that Michelle's father expected too much of Michelle.

"I thought he was pushing pretty hard, but she started to

move to whatever level she was playing at. She started to play to that level," says Nakama. "So it looked like she could handle it on her own. If she couldn't handle it, then they would've had some type of feedback from her and resistance from her. But she seemed to enjoy it, she seemed to enjoy the competition, working that hard, so it worked out."

It's a question Michelle hears often in interviews: "Do you feel your parents have pushed you too hard?" Her answer: "I wouldn't really call it 'pushing,' because they didn't really push me that much. It was more self-motivated."

Personally, Nakama might have chosen a different path for Michelle: "I wanted her to compete and dominate the women and the juniors. They've kind of skipped some steps here, and that is really not the traditional way of winning and dominating. Only time will tell to see how that affects her in winning golf tournaments."

FAST FACT

When Michelle was just eleven years old, she got invited to appear on Jay Leno, but she turned down the invitation!

That nontraditional path is something that comes up time and again, because it is such a unique situation. Nakama was right; Michelle did skip some steps. Rather than join the AJGA (American Junior Golf Association)—the national golf organization for teens—building a résumé of golf accomplishments, Michelle went about things a different way. She began competing against adults not at age seventeen or eighteen, like most golfers, but at age twelve. And as you'll read in the next chapter, she played in her first LPGA event, something most women golfers don't do until after college, at just twelve years old.

But the Wies might have done a few things differently, too, had they been allowed. They would have liked for Michelle to play in AJGA events and gain that valuable national competitive experience, but the age limit at that time was thirteen. At age ten, Michelle was ready to play high-level competition, but the AJGA didn't make an exception to their age requirement just for her. So she simply qualified for and played in adult events instead. And won. By the time she hit the AJGA's thirteen-year-old age requirement, she had already tasted victory among adults, and by then there was no looking back.

3

Stepping Up

Golf is partly natural, but most of
it is practice. You have to work so
hard at it. Some of it comes
easily, but other things don't
come easily at all.

Michelle was beginning to run out of competition; she had beaten all of Hawaii's best amateurs—male and female, junior and adult. Her parents decided it was time she tried golf on a bigger stage—the LPGA.

THE TAKEFUJI CLASSIC

In February of 2002, the seventh-grader attempted to qualify for her first LPGA event, the Takefuji Classic. It was a good choice of tournaments because it was being played in her own backyard— at the Waikoloa Beach Resort on the Big Island of Hawaii. She would be accustomed to the course and the conditions.

At the Monday qualifier (see the following sidebar), in rain and 30-mile-an-hour winds, Michelle shot an 83. Fellow ama-

What Is a Monday Qualifier?

Most LPGA tournaments are open only to members of the LPGA, and amateur players have no chance of gaining entry. However, some tournaments reserve a couple of spots for amateurs and other nonmembers. To win one of the spots, golfers with a handicap of 3.4 or less can play an event called a Monday qualifier. On the Monday before the tournament begins, these players tee it up, with the top two golfers winning a spot in the field. This is one of the ways tournament organizers and sponsors ensure that spots are taken only by the best golfers, while giving non–LPGA members the opportunity to compete.

teur Sally Soranaka was the only player to beat her, with a 79. The 83 would be enough to guarantee Michelle a spot in the 132-player field and the honor of becoming, at age twelve, the youngest female to qualify for an LPGA event.

So what was it like, her first experience playing with pros? According to her coach and caddie for the event, Casey Nakama, Michelle was full of nerves. "At the time we were just excited to be playing in an LPGA event. During the tournament I was just trying to keep her calm because it was the first time with a gallery and it was the first time we were behind the ropes," he says. It was a very big deal, playing right alongside the best women golfers in the world—women whom Michelle normally saw only on television.

On Thursday, the first day of the actual tournament, the wind calmed down and Michelle was able to make an even-par 72. The next day she shot a 74—not quite good enough to

What Does It Mean to "Miss the Cut"?

After the first two rounds of a professional golf tournament (usually played on a Thursday and Friday), the bottom half of the field (the group of competitors) is eliminated. Those unfortunate players have "missed the cut" and are out of the tournament. Only the top half of the field advances to the weekend rounds.

Miss the cut and you get nothing, while those who make the cut split the prize money (unless they're amateurs, who don't play for money). The better you do, the more money you make.

Only one woman has ever made the cut in a PGA Tour tournament—that was Babe Didrikson Zaharias, who accomplished the feat three times back in 1945. Since Babe, only a few women have played in PGA Tour events (Annika Sorenstam, Suzy Whaley, and Michelle). But none have yet made the cut. As of this writing, Michelle has played in four PGA Tour events and has not yet made the cut in any of them. But keep in mind it took Tiger Woods eight tries to make his first cut! His first attempt was at the Nissan Los Angeles Open, when he was sixteen years old. He missed the cut by six strokes. The first time he made a PGA Tour cut was at the 1995 Masters, when he was nineteen. He tied for forty-first place. Two years later, he won it.

place in the top 50 percent of the field—and she missed the cut (see the sidebar above). With the calm conditions, the professionals with whom she was playing were able to go low—Annika Sorenstam ended up winning the tournament with a score of 14-under-par. Although Michelle didn't make the cut, her first LPGA experience taught her a lot about professional-level golf and where she fit in.

For one thing, as she warmed up on the driving range she noticed that she, at twelve years old, could hit the ball just as far as or farther than the best female golfers in the world. Nakama recalls that her drives earned her an audience: "At that time, her swing was functioning really well. When we stood on the range and hit some balls, the LPGA women stopped and they were watching her. For twelve years old she was really impressive." Watching your ball fly right past a pro's—talk about a confidence builder!

Playing in the Takefuji Classic taught Michelle how challenging LPGA events could be. "I had lots of fun, but it was tougher than I thought," Michelle said to the press after the

Someone Please Explain Golf Scores

Most PGA Tour and LPGA golf tournaments include four rounds of golf, played over four days. That's why you'll often see tournament scores reported like this: 72-70-71-69. Each number represents one day's score.

Scores are written relative to par, the number a good golfer should make on each hole. On a par 4, for example, it should take a good golfer four strokes to get the ball in the hole—two to reach the green, plus two putts. Courses have par, too—most courses are par 72s. If a player scored a 75, which is three strokes higher than 72, their score would be recorded as "plus three." If they scored, say, a 68, their score would be marked for that day as "four under" (meaning four strokes under par).

tournament. "Maybe because I was thinking more than I should. The competition here is way different. They're more consistent and you have to be on the fairway. Every shot counts."

A NEW COACH

February of 2002 was a big month for Michelle. Not only did she qualify for her first LPGA event, but she was also introduced to someone who would play a large role in her life: It was Gary Gilchrist, a teaching professional with the David Leadbetter Golf Academy in Bradenton, Florida (see the sidebar on page 38), who would wind up coaching Michelle for the next three years.

One of Gilchrist's roles at the Leadbetter Academy was recruiting new junior talent. He, like many people, had heard of the twelve-year-old whiz kid's successes in Hawaii. At that point, Michelle had won the Hawaii State Women's Golf Association Stroke Play Championship, then the Jennie K. Wilson Invitational, a tournament for amateur women. She'd also been the youngest woman to qualify for the U.S. Women's Amateur Public Links and now, after the Takefuji Classic, was the youngest to qualify for an LPGA event.

In January, she had teed it up with PGA Tour professionals at a six-hole exhibition match and earned her nickname—the Big Wiesy—from veteran pro Tom Lehman. Lehman saw the same easy fluidity in Michelle's swing that PGA Tour champion Ernie Els—the Big Easy—was famous for. "She looks like Ernie Els when she swings," explained Lehman. "And her golf swing is perfect—it's perfect! Her poise is unbelievable. You either have it or you don't, and this girl has got it."

Nicknames

Don't underestimate the power of a good nickname. In the sports world, nicknames can be an indication that an athlete has made it. Some famous nicknames: Jack Nicklaus is known as the "Golden Bear." Ernie Els is, of course, "the Big Easy." LPGA star Paula Creamer also goes by "the Pink Panther." And two of golf's legends were born "Eldrick" and "Mildred." No wonder Tiger Woods and Babe Didrikson used nicknames!

So Gilchrist set out to Hawaii to meet this little girl who had caught the attention of so many. "My responsibility was to build a junior program from the ground up, and I said from the beginning, the quickest way to develop a program is to go out into the junior golf world and meet people out there, and build relationships and inspire them to come to the academy to train," he recalls. "I was the person who took the initiative to go to Hawaii and meet the family back when I was hearing so much about her from the PGA Tour players, like Tom Lehman calling her the Big Wiesy."

At their first meeting, Gilchrist reports, Michelle let it drop over lunch that her goal was to someday play on both tours—the LPGA and the PGA—as well as in the Masters. "That's great, but do you have what it takes?" asked Gilchrist. After lunch, they went out to the range together. Michelle took a swing, and Gilchrist had his answer.

"After the first swing, I knew that she could do it," Gilchrist says. "I was standing there, and I meant nothing to her; it was just the joy of looking at the target and making that swing. I've

How Would You Like to Go to Golf School?

Imagine going to a school where you do homework half the day, then play golf the other half: "Okay, kids, today we're going to work on English, biology, and your short game."

You might have heard about the DLGA—the David Leadbetter Golf Academy. It offers just such an education. It's actually part of a larger umbrella of sports academies run by IMG—the International Management Group—that also includes centers for learning baseball, basketball, and tennis.

The schools are situated together on a 170-acre campus in Bradenton, Florida. Along with all the sports schools, there's also a K–12 boarding school called Pendleton. Students live there year-round, taking classes and working on their chosen sport. Everything is geared toward maximizing each student's athletic abilities—even cafeteria meals are carefully planned by a nutrition expert, with athletic performance in mind.

The DLGA's goal is to produce "students who can play," rather than merely swing a club. To that end, the academy provides swing coaching, of course, but also mental and physical conditioning, course management, and tournament preparation. They work on all areas of a player's game. The school accepts students of all abilities, although its claim to fame is its elite athletes.

It's not just youngsters who come to the DLGA; professional golfers come to the academy for coaching advice from David Leadbetter, too. Why Leadbetter? He's considered by many to be the world's best golf coach, and he's certainly one of the best-known. He's worked with PGA Tour professionals including Ernie Els, Tom Watson, Greg Norman, Nick Price, Nick Faldo, Justin Rose, Charles Howell III, Ian Poulter, and many others. He's also written a bunch of best-sellers about the golf swing and contributes to *Golf Digest* magazine.

Originally from Worthing, in Sussex, England, Leadbetter started as a competitive golfer himself, playing on the South African and European tours. But he found teaching the game to be more satisfying than playing it and began a career in instruction. Now there are twenty-seven Leadbetter Academies around the world, with hundreds of instructors teaching his method. Before he moved on to the International Junior Golf Academy in South Carolina in 2004, Gary Gilchrist (Michelle's coach) was a top instructor at the DLGA. Now Michelle works with Leadbetter himself.

Golf school doesn't come cheap, however. Full-time tuition at Leadbetter Academy will set you back about $45,000 a year, and a single private lesson will run you about $225 an hour.

been around golf since I was six years old. I played with Vijay Singh when I was playing in South Africa; I've seen some of the world's best players. And I watched this girl at twelve years old swing a club, and it was like nothing I'd seen before."

The range was 265 yards long, and Michelle's drives flew right over the fence. Gilchrist couldn't believe it. That's when he knew that he had a special talent on his hands; the next step was talking her into training at his school.

Most students at the Leadbetter Academy move to Florida and live at the school, taking lessons while completing their regular schoolwork. This wasn't going to work for the Wies, however, who had no interest in leaving Hawaii. BJ's academic career was well established at the University of Hawaii, and Bo was successful in Honolulu's lucrative real estate business. Besides all of that, the family was very satisfied with the education Michelle was receiving at the Punahou School. Even though Gilchrist offered Michelle a full scholarship to the David Leadbetter Academy, including room, board, and all training, the Wies didn't budge.

So they worked out a compromise. "When we had that meeting, I knew they'd never leave Hawaii," says Gilchrist. "They loved Hawaii, so I didn't try and sell them on moving to Bradenton. I sold them on coming there and taking lessons from me and helping improve her there."

Thus began frequent trips to the mainland. Starting in May of that year, Michelle and her parents would take the long series of flights to Florida every school break for Michelle to spend a few weeks getting instruction at the Leadbetter Academy. They ended up becoming so close to Gilchrist that he even traveled with them for her big tournaments, sometimes caddying. He became, as he put it, a "member of the family."

And as an adopted family member, Gilchrist noted that her family was absolutely critical to Michelle's development as a player: "Her parents would come with her every day. It's one thing to say you need to spend quality time with your kids; it's another thing doing it on a day-to-day basis. She feels so secure and loved, and supported, in a positive way."

Every competition, and every practice, Michelle's parents would accompany her to the course. They would sit next to her as she hit balls on the range, offering tips in Korean, and stand nearby during her lessons. Some coaches might find this annoying or distracting, but not Gilchrist. "When she got to be

Who's Your Caddie?

What is a caddie, anyway? And why would you need one? Professional golfers hire caddies for several reasons. The most obvious function is to carry the player's golf bag. But caddies do other things, too—they're like a personal assistant on the golf course. They scout the course, measure yardages, read greens, rake bunkers, and make recommendations for golf shots. This makes things easier for the golfer—they can focus on making a good shot, rather than all those details that might distract them. Caddies are also responsible for the player's equipment—they clean clubs, keep track of them, and help the player get to the right place at the right time. A good caddie can make the difference between winning and losing a golf tournament.

At the time of the Takefuji Classic, Michelle hadn't had a caddie other than her father. Because it was a professional golf tournament—her first one—the Wies decided it would be a good idea to have Casey Nakama on her bag.

Since the Takefuji in 2002, Michelle has had many caddies. Normally caddies get paid via the golfer's earnings—they receive 10 percent of a professional golfer's winnings (so they have a vested interest in the golfer's success).

When Michelle played as an amateur, meaning she received no money no matter how well she played, she had to hire caddies for a flat rate, usually around one thousand dollars. That's why they often used her father or coach as a caddie, rather than hiring one.

fifteen years old, she was old enough to take instruction and the parents could step away a little bit. But when she was twelve years old, the farthest they would stand from her was about 3 to 4 feet. They were always there, making sure she was okay, she was happy, she was understanding what she was doing," Gilchrist recalls.

Others have noted their closeness as a family unit as well. Lily Yao, a friend and mentor to Michelle who's known the family for years, says, "They're very close; they do things all together, as one." Family friend Linda Johnston told *Fortune* magazine, "I have never seen a family so close. It's almost like they are one person." Michelle herself told the press at one point, "We're so close, we go everywhere together. We think the same way because we've been together so long."

Thinking alike is something Gilchrist sees as an advantage: "Being around her parents, she was very mature. She thought very logically, like her parents. And she played like a child. That combination makes a Tiger Woods. With Tiger Woods, it's the same thing. His mother was very firm and taught him values, and taught him responsibility and taught him how to be accountable. And his father taught him how to be mentally tough." Gilchrist attributes much of Michelle's maturity and mental focus to her relationship with her parents. Spending that much time with a college professor has to rub off after a while, after all.

SO WHAT DID Gilchrist teach Michelle? He focused first on her grip—the way she held the club in her hands (see the following sidebar). He had her go from a strong grip to a neutral one, so that the clubface would be square when it hit the ball. "What I try to explain to every student is that the key to build-

Get a Grip!

What's all this about strong or neutral grips? No, a strong grip isn't what it sounds like—it does not mean you hold the club tighter. Rather, a strong grip means that as the player (a right-handed player) is holding a club, the left wrist is angled so that the top of the hand is facing up. With a weak grip, the top of the left hand faces toward the ground. With a neutral grip, the top of the hand faces out toward the target. Such a small detail doesn't sound like it would make much difference, but actually it does. As Gilchrist pointed out, the way a golfer holds the club determines the direction the ball will travel.

ing a good golf swing always comes from fundamentals," says Gilchrist. "Because what creates direction is the clubface, and what creates the face is the grip. What controls good body motion is good posture; what controls posture is good alignment. So working on grip, posture, and alignment would create a better plane in her swing and make her more consistent."

Gilchrist also focused on physical fitness. He had his work cut out for him—Michelle was notoriously anti-exercise. As a small child, she had selected golf over other sports because she hated running. At one point Casey Nakama even offered to run with her every morning to help her get in shape. But she always refused. "I told her, these girls you're playing against at these big tournaments, they're all going to be in shape, they'll have an advantage over you. But she wouldn't do it," says Nakama.

"Back then she was very closed-minded when it came to training," Gilchrist laughs. "In PE class, running around the school once was enough for her. But with golfers today, it's all about stability, lower-body stability. With women golfers, you have to work on their arm strength, shoulders, and midsection." Under Gilchrist's guidance, Michelle finally began working out regularly, riding a stationary bike and working her "core"—the muscles that make up the abdominals, lower back, obliques, and hips.

Gilchrist had a pretty clear philosophy when it came to Michelle's instruction: "What I wanted to do was teach her the angles of the game. My philosophy is to work on a technical part, then on feel. Then I would challenge her in competition, so she could take what she learned to the golf course. We worked on every area, different shots, chipping out of thick rough, flop shots. You had to keep her challenged all the time; otherwise she would lose interest."

One of the ways he would keep her motivated was a simple trick: bribery. "Make this putt and you get five dollars," he would tell her. "Put this shot in the hole and we go to your favorite restaurant for dinner." This was a motivational tool her parents had been using for years, and Gilchrist found it just as successful as they had.

Gilchrist also had to pry her away from her favorite club— her driver. "She had this Fujikura 7-degree driver, that Tiger might be able to hit," Gilchrist recalls. "And she used to give it the biggest, longest swing ever. And that's what created some of her tendencies in her swing. But she loved her driver because it went far."

Yes, it did. At that point Michelle could hit drives farther than 300 yards. Keep in mind that the average recreational female golfer drives closer to 160 yards. At just thirteen years old, Michelle could already hit the ball as far as a PGA Tour professional. Not every time, of course, but even being able to hit that far occasionally made her stand out.

But Gilchrist knew that hitting a long ball wasn't going to be enough. Michelle would have to learn accuracy as well and master plenty of other shots to make up for the trouble that her driver might put her into. "On the golf course, power players don't usually hit too many fairways, so you have to teach them how to hit out of long rough. Tiger, Phil Mickelson, Ernie Els—most long drivers don't rank high in driving accuracy," Gilchrist explains.

Physical fitness, nutrition, different types of shots, and putting—these were the things Gilchrist had Michelle work on. And like Casey Nakama, Gilchrist found Michelle to be an apt student. Show her a shot, and she would have it down by the next day.

MICHELLE'S GOLF GAME wasn't the only thing that was changing—as she found more and more success on the golf course, she found something else, too: celebrity. At just twelve years old, she became the subject of a PGA TV special that aired on the USA Network and was interviewed for profiles in some of golf's biggest print publications—from *Golf for Women* to *Golf Magazine.*

All that attention could have gone to her head, but her parents tried to keep her life as normal as possible. As BJ pointed out to *Golf Today,* "Being a young golf star is different from being a young star in Hollywood, or in music. She likes movies, reading, music. She makes good grades, and since she mostly plays in tournaments during summer vacation, she only misses a couple of weeks of school. She's been able to handle all the attention and is having a normal childhood. The only difference is, she plays golf."

Michelle had the ability to turn off that golf switch; she could be mature and focused while playing yet still enjoy all the things that come with childhood when she finished her round. As Gilchrist put it, "Michelle is like twenty-four years old on the golf course, but then she'll come off the course and turn into a thirteen-year-old. She loves DVDs; she loves music; she loves dogs. She loves to be social; her friends at school love her to death. She has an outgoing personality."

FAST FACT
Michelle's favorite golf club: her driver

After three trips to Bradenton and continuing to practice at home nearly every day, Michelle won her second straight Hawaii State Junior Golf Association's Tournament of Champions. Then, playing in the Women's, rather than the Junior, Division of the Hawaii State Open, she won the title, shooting 8-under-par and crushing the field by thirteen strokes.

Winning the Hawaii State Open by such a large margin was an impressive feat for a twelve-year-old and showed just how far she'd come. But it wasn't quite enough for her; though she was proud of her accomplishment, she and her family felt that she was ready for a bigger stage. It was time to go national.

FAST FACT
Michelle speaks several languages: She speaks English and Korean fluently and a little bit of Japanese.

4

Victory

I'm happy out of my mind. I like
beating a lot of people.

The year was 2003, and Michelle Wie, the thirteen-year-old whiz kid from Hawaii who had won just about every amateur event her home state had to offer, the girl who had declared that she wanted to someday play in the Masters, was winless.

No, not literally winless, of course—she'd won plenty of local events. But on the national level, Michelle had yet to declare a victory. Enter the U.S. Women's Amateur Public Links. Michelle had played in it before—in fact, she had been the youngest woman ever to qualify for it at age ten. But up to now, she hadn't made it past the semifinals. After years of training with her local coach, Casey Nakama, and frequent trips to Florida to work with Gary Gilchrist, her coach at the David Leadbetter Golf Academy, she was ready to step it up a notch.

Early in 2003, Michelle had played in the LPGA's Kraft Nabisco Championship (a major) and not only made her first LPGA cut but also tied for ninth place. She became the youngest player ever to make an LPGA cut, and her 66 in the third round tied the record for an amateur (of any age) playing in a major. Had she been a professional, she would have taken home $35,000.

Michelle's game had come a long way in the past year.

Only thirteen years old at this point, she already stood six feet tall—a huge asset for golfers. Her height was something her coaches could use to her advantage, and they worked with her on using that leverage to create extra power.

At the Kraft Nabisco, Michelle drove an average of 286 yards—one of the longest drives on the LPGA Tour. According to her coach, Casey Nakama, Michelle was swinging her best as the summer of 2003 began, and she was ready to hit the first tee at the U.S. Women's Amateur Public Links Championship.

What is the U.S. Women's Amateur Public Links? The USGA (United States Golf Association, golf's governing body here in the U.S.) sponsors thirteen championships each year, one of which is the Women's Public Links (or Publinx, for short). The tournament began in 1977, and it's a little different from the others; it's called "Public Links" because it's not open to everyone, only to female amateurs who play on public golf courses. If you belong to a private country club, you're out.

The tournament has a unique format with three stages: First come the qualifiers. Every player who wants to enter this tournament has to first win her spot, proving her mettle through several days of qualifying play. Then comes the actual tournament, which begins with two days of stroke play. Every stroke is counted, and at the end of the two days half the field—sixty-four players—move on to the next stage of the tournament and the other half goes home.

The next and final stage of the tournament is match play. Players go head-to-head in individual matches, with only the

Match Play Versus Stroke Play: What's the Difference?

Most professional tournaments use a format called stroke play. Each player keeps track of the number of strokes they take on each hole; then at the end of the round the player with the lowest number of strokes wins. Over a four-round tournament, for example, a player might shoot 70-69-72-68, for a total of 279, beating everyone who shot higher than 279.

In match play, however, the overall number of strokes doesn't matter—what matters is who wins the most holes. Players pair up, and whoever gets the lowest number of strokes on a hole wins the hole. Say one person makes a four and the other makes a five. The one who made the four wins the hole. The winner of the match is the person who wins the most holes (holes with ties don't count). The winner of the tournament is the player who wins the most matches.

That might not sound like a big difference, but it is. For one thing, in match play players often don't have to finish all eighteen holes. One person might be so dominant that they win the first ten holes in a row. There's no way the other person can win at that point, because even if they won the next eight, they would still lose the match. So the match ends right there.

There's also a difference in the way the scores are described. A stroke play winner is said to have won "by three strokes," for example. A match play win, however, might be described as "4 and 3." That means the winner was four holes ahead with three holes left to play. The match would be over after just fifteen holes, in other words. You might also hear that someone won a match "1 up." That means that after eighteen holes, one of the players won by one hole. If the match is "all square" (tied) after eighteen hole, the players proceed to a play-off.

In match play, a player often concedes putts to the other player, meaning that their ball is close enough to the hole that the opponent doesn't make them bother putting it out. "That's good," a player will say, allowing the other player to pick up their ball. No one ever pockets their ball before putting out during stroke play.

It's not just scoring that's different between stroke and match play—strategy is different, too. In stroke play, a player is battling the course. Competitors try not to think about what their opponents are doing but simply focus on their own game. In match play, it's your opponent and only your opponent that matters. Players battle one another, not the course. If your opponent hits a good drive, you'd better pull out your driver and match it. But if they hit a drive out-of-bounds, you can relax and play conservatively.

Match play is classic competitive golf—the way the game was originally meant to be played.

winner of each match advancing to play the winners of the other matches. The field gets whittled down, finally, to just two players. The finalists (the last two standing) then play thirty-six holes of golf to determine who will be the winner of the overall tournament. Not counting the qualifiers, the tournament is six full days long, a grueling test of skill and endurance.

Victory

At her regional qualifiers, Michelle shot well enough to join the 144-member field at the par-72, 6,068-yard Ocean Hammock Golf Club in Palm Coast, Florida. During the two rounds of stroke play, Michelle hung in there with the best of them, shooting 73-71 to place third.

On Thursday, the first day of match play, Michelle Wie beat Jane Rah, of Torrance, California, 2 and 1.

The next morning, during the second round of match play, Michelle ended up meeting none other than Hwanhee Lee, the woman who had knocked Michelle out of the tournament the year before. Michelle wasn't worried, though. "My game is a lot better than last year," she told the press. "It's a whole new and different day, so anything can happen."

On the fourteenth hole, a 487-yard par 5, Michelle was down two holes. She had only five holes left to make up the deficit and possibly pull ahead. She hit a 282-yard drive down the right side of the fairway, then hit a 3 iron 205 yards over water onto the green with her second shot. Lee, who had hit her drive into water, then into a bunker, conceded the hole to Michelle, not making her hit her 4-foot eagle putt.

On the next hole, Michelle squared the match with a birdie, then followed that up with a par to Lee's bogey. Now Michelle was one up. If she won the next hole, she would win the match. Losing the hole would mean the pair would go into the eighteenth hole all square and Michelle would possibly face a play-off. She didn't have to worry, though. She won the next hole with a par and won the match 2 and 1. In just four holes of golf, she had gone from a two-hole deficit to a two-hole advantage.

But there was no time to rest or to celebrate. She had another match that same afternoon, against Mayumi Motoyama of Littleton, Colorado. The lack of rest caught up to Michelle, though, and she ended up with a bloody nose—something that occasionally happens when she's tired. In spite of her fatigue, Michelle swept the match, 5 and 4. Saturday would bring the quarterfinals—another long day of golf. It began in the morning when Michelle faced Becky Lucidi, the reigning U.S. Women's Amateur champion. Michelle wasn't intimidated and made quick work of Lucidi, beating her 6 and 5—an enormous winning margin.

The afternoon brought another round—the semifinals. This time Michelle would face another teenager, Aimee Cho of Orlando, Florida. Michelle started strong and never let up. With her father carrying her bag, Michelle played smart and conservatively, teeing off with a 4 wood rather than a driver, being sure to keep the ball in play. She didn't want to have to come back from a deficit the way she had the day before against Hwanhee Lee. Michelle's strategy worked, as she eagled number 4 and birdied number 6. She won five of the first six holes, and went on to win 5 and 4.

THE FINALS

Michelle had now won five consecutive matches and played seven consecutive rounds. Only one more stood between her and the title. It was going to be a particularly tough one, however, since it would comprise thirty-six straight holes of tournament golf against Virada Nirapathpongporn, the twenty-one-year-old Duke Women's NCAA champion from Thailand who had taken first place during stroke play.

Until that point, Nirapathpongporn had been cutting a swath

through the field, winning her matches with ample comfort room. She wasn't going to make things easy for Michelle.

By the eighth hole of the final thirty-six-hole match against Michelle, Nirapathpongporn was already four up. Even though Michelle had birdied the second hole, Nirapathpongporn answered by birdying five of the next six holes. She was on fire.

But Michelle had some birdies in her bag, too. She made four birdies herself to square the match through eighteen holes.

They began the afternoon round exactly where they had started—all square. Except for one thing: Michelle had changed into a red shirt, just like Tiger Woods for his Sunday rounds.

Again, Nirapathpongporn started off strong. She took advantage of a few of Michelle's errant shots to go two up. But again Michelle pulled four birdies to swing the match two holes in the other direction.

At the thirty-second hole, a par 5, Michelle decided it was time to turn on the turbo. While most players take three strokes to reach the green on a par 5, Michelle went for it with her second shot, hitting over a palm tree. She landed on the green, 20 feet from the hole; then, with eight hundred spectators cheering, she made the putt for a stunning eagle to go one up.

But Nirapathpongporn fought her way back, so that going into the thirty-fifth hole the two were all square once again. After all that, only two holes would ultimately determine the outcome of the championship.

Any golfer will tell you that winning a golf tournament takes a huge amount of effort along with a fair amount of luck. For Michelle, the luck came at the thirty-fifth hole. Michelle made her par, and Nirapathpongporn, with just a 3-foot putt to halve the hole, missed the putt. That put Michelle one up, with one to play.

On the thirty-sixth and final hole, Michelle stood at the tee box determined to play smart. The time to take risks had passed; now it was time to play safe. She made par, as did Nirapathpongporn, and the roller-coaster ride was finally over. Michelle had won.

She later told Guy Yocom of *Golf Digest* a little secret about that moment on the thirty-fifth green: "The match was all square, and I made my putt. Now she had to make her three-footer. What I've never told a writer before is I wear a pendant on my neck with Mary on it. When I have an important shot to make, I sometimes hold it in my hand and say a little prayer. It always works. This time I held the pendant and said a prayer that she'd miss the putt. And she did miss, and I wound up winning. It made me wonder, though—is that the type of thing I should pray for?"

"I think it will probably be one of the most memorable matches that I've played," Nirapathpongporn says now. "Michelle put on a great show. I really enjoyed it; I just came out one shot short. But it was great playing with her. She's everything everyone talked about."

"It means a lot," Michelle told the press after the Publinx. "I never won a national championship. The Women's Amateur Public Links was my first for everything. It was my first national tournament to play in, when I was ten, so I'm pretty glad."

It was a painful loss for Virada, but don't feel too bad for her. The very next month she won the 2003 U.S. Women's Amateur title, avenging her loss the best way possible—with a national championship of her own.

Until this win, Michelle had been a local sensation known

Player Profile: Virada Nirapathpongporn

Michelle's win over Virada Nirapathpongporn was no small accomplishment. Virada, who goes by the nickname Oui (that's pronounced "oo-wee"), was a formidable opponent. At the time she played against Michelle at the U.S. Women's Amateur Public Links, she was something of a star herself.

She was the 2002 NCAA champion and a First-Team All-American from 2001 to 2004, not to mention a three-time Academic All-American. She had also played in the Kraft Nabisco Championship earlier that year along with Michelle, tying for twenty-first.

According to her coach at Duke, Dan Brooks, Oui is meticulous, exacting, and an extremely hard worker. "Oui is a master of the game; she's not someone who thinks about the person she's playing against and wants to drill somebody," says Brooks, who still works with Nirapathpongporn as her swing coach. "That's not Oui. Oui is more of an artist. Golf is a game to master; you work on it your whole life, learn every shot that you can. To me, that's the best way to play the game."

Nirapathpongporn grew up in Thailand; her father, a surgeon, taught her the game when she was eight years old. She moved to Australia at age fifteen, then to the United States to work with David Leadbetter at his famed golf academy. She's had to play through adversity—her father passed away in 2004 of leukemia, which he had fought for years. It was a stunning blow for Virada, who was very close with her father, but she has managed to remain steady.

Coach Brooks credits her loss to Michelle as the driving

force that enabled Virada to win the next month at the U.S. Women's Amateur: "What Oui needed was to get a little bit angry. And I think that's what came from that, playing that good against Michelle Wie and have it not happen at the end. That loss really got under her skin and propelled her at the U.S. Amateur. She was a little bit more grown-up by the time she got to the U.S. Amateur. She was a different person. She was going to get it done."

Now you are able to watch Oui on the LPGA—she just earned a spot for the '06 season, after grinding out a second-place spot on the developmental Futures Tour last year. Keep your eye on her; she'll be a force to reckon with.

only in Hawaii; now the whole world became aware of this thirteen-year-old who had made history at the Women's Publinx. She went from a curiosity to a legitimate competitor, almost overnight.

And the U.S. Women's Amateur Publinx was only one stop on her twenty-thousand-mile odyssey that summer. Michelle's schedule was packed: Before starting school again in August, she also played in the LPGA's ShopRite Classic, the U.S. Women's Open, the USGA Girl's Junior, the U.S. Women's Amateur, the LPGA's Jamie Farr Kroger Classic, and, finally, the Canadian Tour's Bay Mills Open Players Championship, a men's event.

It was by far her busiest schedule to date. But she and her family loved it—they enjoyed spending so much time together, traveling around, staying in hotels. To Michelle, it was an adventure. To her parents, it was a break from their usual routine and a wonderful chance to support their daughter in achieving her dreams. And afterward, when she finally got home, she received her biggest thrill of all—her math teacher asked for her autograph.

WHAT IS THE USGA? HOW IS IT DIFFERENT FROM THE LPGA OR THE PGA?

You might have noticed that some tournaments are PGA events, some are LPGA, and then others, like the U.S. Women's Amateur Public Links mentioned in this chapter, are USGA events. What's the difference?

First of all, the LPGA and PGA (Ladies Professional Golf Association and Professional Golfers' Association, respectively) are not just organizations; they're tours. Players gain member-

How to Join the USGA

You might not have the game to join the LPGA or the PGA, but you can join the USGA anytime. Here's how: Call their Member Services Line at 800-223-0041 and ask them to send you an application, or go to www.usga.org and apply directly online. Once you join, they'll send you a copy of the Rules of Golf, a personalized bag tag for your golf bag, an ID card, a U.S. Open hat, and the ability to establish your handicap. You'll also get a monthly newsletter and priority for purchasing tickets to USGA tournaments. Anyone can join the USGA—it costs fifteen dollars, and you don't have to be a golf pro or even a player.

ship to the tours through their play, usually through a lengthy annual tournament called Q-School, or Qualifying School. Once you're a member, you literally tour around the country, playing events that are run by that Tour.

The PGA Tour holds forty-eight official tournaments around the country each year and offers more than $250 million in prize money. It is the most prestigious golf tour around, claiming the best golfers in the world. The LPGA Tour holds thirty-four tournaments each year, scattered all around the country. It was founded in 1950, which makes it the oldest women's professional sports organization in the country.

Don't confuse the PGA Tour with the PGA of America, a separate organization. (Yes, two PGAs. Are you confused yet?) The PGA of America began in 1916, when a department store magnate, Rodman Wanamaker, founded the nonprofit association to help grow the game of golf. It has since become the largest working sports organization in the world, with more than twenty-eight thousand members. Anyone can join who works in the game of golf, including not just touring pros but also club professionals and instructors.

The PGA Tour began when the Tournament Players Division split from the PGA of America in 1968. The group of players hired their own commissioner and began running their own events in order to have control over their tournament schedule. The two organizations work closely together on many events, however, and most touring pros are members of both groups.

Most of the professional golfers you've heard of are members of either the LPGA or the PGA Tour, from Annika Sorenstam to Tiger Woods. They have a unique life, traveling from

Do You Want to Go to a USGA Event?

The USGA handles ticketing to only three of their events—
the U.S. Open, the U.S. Women's Open, and the U.S. Senior
Open. Contact the USGA at 800-698-0661 or send an e-mail
to ticketquestions@usga.org to receive ticket applications.
Word of warning: Tickets to the "main event"—the U.S.
Open—generally sell out very early, usually more than a year
in advance.

Tickets to the other ten of their events (open only to amateurs) are handled by the clubs that host the tournaments.
Many of them have no cover charge. Visit www.usga.org to
find a list of all the annual USGA tournaments.

one city to the next each week, playing in the various tournaments. They earn their living by playing for the prize money
offered at each tournament and through their sponsorships.

The PGA Tour and the LPGA Tour aren't the only tours
around—in the United States there's also the Nationwide Tour
and the Futures Tour (which are developmental tours for the
PGA and the LPGA; see the sidebar on page 60), the Champions Tour (reserved for pros aged fifty and older), and several
"mini-tours." Worldwide you'll find the European Tour, the
Japan PGA, the Canadian Tour, the South African PGA, and
many more.

So now you know the difference between the LPGA and the
PGA. Let's take a look at the USGA—the United States Golf Association.

Futures Tour? Nationwide Tour? What're They?

Say your lifelong dream is to play on the LPGA, but you're not quite good enough. You need a little bit more competitive experience. One option is to play on the Futures Tour (officially known as the Duramed FUTURES Tour). It's the LPGA's official developmental tour, grooming golfers the same way minor league baseball prepares players for the big leagues.

Founded in 1981, the Futures Tour holds eighteen or nineteen tournaments annually, with average purses of around seventy-five thousand dollars. Sounds like small potatoes compared to the LPGA's average purse size of around $1.4 million, but what players gain in experience on the Futures Tour can be more valuable than money—each year, the top-five money winners on the Futures Tour automatically get their LPGA card.

Futures Tour alumni include LPGA members such as Cristie Kerr, Karrie Webb, Laura Davies, Rosie Jones, Grace Park, Meg Mallon, Dottie Pepper, and Lorena Ochoa—all champions on the LPGA.

The Nationwide Tour plays the same role for the PGA Tour. It's changed names a few times since its inception in 1990 (it started as the Ben Hogan Tour, then became the Nike Tour, then the Buy.com tour, and finally the Nationwide Tour). It holds around thirty tournaments each year. The top twenty-one money winners "graduate" to the PGA Tour. Alumni include Ernie Els, Jim Furyk, David Duval, John Daly, Tom Lehman, and Stuart Appleby.

The USGA is the oldest of these organizations—it began in 1894, when its founding members decided it was time for the United States to have its own centralized body for writing the rules of golf and conducting championships. Until that time, the Royal and Ancient Golf Club of St. Andrews, Scotland's famed group, had been golf's only governing body. The USGA now operates thirteen championships each year, ten of which are held exclusively for amateurs. The U.S. Open, the Women's U.S. Open, and the Senior U.S. Open are the three championships that allow professionals to enter. They're called Opens because of the fact that they are open to anyone who is good enough to qualify—amateurs and professionals alike.

FAST FACT

If Michelle had been allowed to keep the money, she would have earned $57,700 when she was just thirteen years old!

5

Constructive Criticism?

There are some people that are
always against me. But, you know,
I just have to realize that I'm
having a lot of fun, and this is
what I want to do. And I'm not
going to stop just for them.

Michelle's victory at the U.S. Women's Amateur Public Links meant a lot to her; a national championship places a player squarely in the "big leagues." It brought her lots of attention, and with it, lots of scrutiny.

It wasn't just her victory that people noticed; it was the fact that a thirteen-year-old girl was playing among adults rather than juniors her own age. And people couldn't help but notice that something she always mentioned in interviews was her desire to one day play alongside the men as a member of the PGA Tour.

Some people just laughed off this teenager's seemingly impossible dream. But others took a closer look and didn't like what they saw. Here was a girl who was willing to skip not just junior golf, not just amateur golf, but also, apparently, the

LPGA; she wanted to vault right over to play with Tiger Woods and Ernie Els.

How could this be? critics wondered. Why wasn't she taking the traditional path that a golf career generally took: junior tournaments, then amateur tournaments, then, and only then, professional events? Did she think she was too good for that? Were Michelle's parents pushing her toward this goal? Or just being overindulgent? And why, these critics asked, couldn't Michelle stay at one level long enough to dominate there before moving on to the next?

Here was the reason: Michelle's parents felt that what mattered more than simply winning junior tournaments was getting Michelle the best experience possible, so they took a quality-over-quantity approach. The best way to accomplish this was to place her against the highest competition available. Because of her success, she received sponsor exemptions (see sidebar on page 75) to play in professional tournaments—the highest competition there is. To her family, accepting those exemptions was a no-brainer.

It wasn't just the media that questioned the Wies' decisions; Michelle faced a certain amount of resentment from some LPGA players as well, thanks to all those sponsor exemptions. Most of them had, after all, had to "pay their dues" to reach their current status, building a sizable portfolio of junior and amateur wins and qualifying for tournaments. To LPGA players, Michelle appeared to be an upstart, stealing media attention and fanfare for nothing more than extra publicity.

And it wasn't just Michelle's sponsor exemptions that made some women resent her; they also felt offended by her dream to play against men.

Hall of Famer Nancy Lopez, one of the most beloved figures in women's golf, got in on the act, telling reporters that Michelle would be better off playing only against women. "She says she wants to play on the men's tour," said Lopez. "Why? It's a little insulting. She should play out here and try to beat Annika first."

When told of Nancy Lopez's comments, Michelle responded simply, "Well, a lot of people don't know about how I won every [amateur event] in Hawaii, and I can't pay to go to Geneva and play in these kind of events. . . . I mean, you can learn the art of winning out here, too, and that's what I'm trying to do." Michelle was never shy defending her choices.

Michelle's coach, Gary Gilchrist, noted that to his surprise, she seemed to receive better treatment on the PGA Tour than she did at LPGA events. He said, "I found that she was accepted far more by the men [on the PGA Tour] than she was by the LPGA. The men would say, 'Hey, Michelle, we like having you here.' They were a lot warmer out there. A lot of the time we would have one incident after another incident on the LPGA. I would think that a lot of the LPGA would've seen what happened with Tiger Woods and say, 'Here's somebody that's coming on our Tour, who's not taking any of our money and marketing our Tour for free.' I would've treated her a little differently."

STEPPING ON TOES

So what was Gilchrist talking about when he mentioned incidents at LPGA events? To what was he referring? One example is what happened at the 2003 U.S. Women's Open at Pumpkin Ridge Golf Course in North Plains, Oregon. It was just a month after Michelle's victory at the U.S. Women's Amateur

Public Links and her first try at the biggest tournament in women's golf: the U.S. Women's Open.

Michelle was playing with two LPGA professionals, thirty-seven-year-old Danielle Ammaccapane and thirty-one-year-old Tracy Hanson. At that time, Michelle was driving the ball an average of 281 yards. Her partners, however, were averaging only about 240 off the tee. After the threesome teed off, the two LPGA pros would proceed to their balls, roughly on the same spot in the fairway, size up their shots, and hit away. Michelle's ball, however, was another 40 or 50 yards up the fairway.

After her playing partners hit, Michelle would need to make her way up to her ball, pace off her yardage, and consider her club selection before being able to hit, since she was unable to do so while the ladies were sizing up their own shots. This was slowing the threesome down quite a bit, a big no-no in LPGA tournaments that can lead to being "put on the clock" and, ultimately, receiving penalty strokes.

The year before, during the LPGA Wendy's Championship, Michelle had been penalized two strokes for slow play. And she had missed the cut—by two strokes.

Determined not to let this happen again, Michelle and her father, who was caddying for her, began to edge down the fairway while the other two ladies were hitting their balls. The Wies wanted to be sure they had plenty of time to prepare for Michelle's shots, without having to wait for Ammaccapane and Hanson to finish their own. But this wasn't a good solution, either, because the ladies could see Michelle out of the corner of their eyes while they hit. As any golfer knows, catching movement while swinging a club can lead to a poor shot.

To make matters worse, once the group reached the greens,

Don't Walk in My Line!

If you play golf, you know that there are so many rules and regulations, your head will spin from trying to learn them. And aside from the book rules that you're required to know, there are even more unwritten ones that, if you ignore them, can land you in just as hot water. These unwritten rules are referred to as "golf etiquette."

One of Ammaccapane's biggest complaints about Michelle and her father was that they were walking "in her line." What is a line, exactly?

When your ball lands on the putting green, the imaginary line that runs between your ball and the hole is called your line. Walking on or through your playing partner's line is tantamount to punching them in the head. Why? Because Rule 16-1 states that players may not touch the line of a putt, not even to repair scuff marks on the green. A player's golf shoes can leave just such scuff marks on the green's delicate grass—marks that can throw off another player's putt. So walking in someone's line is equivalent to deliberately trying to screw up your partner's putt.

Most golfers know that golf etiquette precludes stepping in another player's line. But on the professional tour, golfers also know they shouldn't step in a player's "through-line," the line that extends past the hole, through which the ball would travel on a come-backer. That through-line was the one Michelle stepped on, which made Ammaccapane so irate.

It's just as important for golfers to be aware of golf etiquette as it is for them to know the rules of golf. Following proper etiquette shows consideration for other players; disregarding it, as Michelle learned the hard way, only leads to problems.

Michelle again tried to speed up play by making her way directly to her ball. At this point, playing partner Ammaccapane got fed up with Michelle's behavior and began berating her for walking "in her line." Most golfers are well aware they should never walk directly in someone's putting line; Ammaccapane was upset that Michelle was walking behind her ball to get to her own, again in Ammaccapane's line of vision.

After the round was over, Ammaccapane left the green before Michelle had finished putting out, and the two did not shake hands.

"The worst was the father," Ammaccapane later told *Golf Digest*. "He wouldn't get pins, couldn't rake a bunker right, kept leaving the bag in the putting line, let his player putt with the flag in. I'm trying to play in the U.S. Open, and I've got Dumb and Dumber over here."

In the scorer's tent after the round, Ammaccapane expressed her frustration at Michelle and her father. Michelle told her father that Ammaccapane said to her, "You are the worst kid I have ever seen playing golf. You will never make it playing this game. I will make money playing golf. You will not."

Ammaccapane's version of the story is a little different. She told *Golf Digest* that what she had said was more like this: "'Michelle, that was the worst etiquette I've ever seen. If you want to be out here, you need to do better.' I didn't get in her face," said Ammaccapane. "I raised my voice a little. I was stern. I let her know I was upset. Yes, she's thirteen, but she doesn't play like she's thirteen, and if you're going to come into this environment, you've got to be ready, and you've got to be prepared to accept all of it."

But even David Fay, executive director of the USGA, likened Ammaccapane to a "drill sergeant." Her comments to Michelle, he said, "had to do with the behavior of her father, and the things he was doing or not doing as a caddie." Fay told *Golf Digest,* "Would Danielle have talked like that to someone else, someone who was forty years old? Probably not, because she might have gotten a fist in the mouth."

Tracy Hanson, who refused to comment about the incident after the round, later agreed with Ammaccapane that BJ was the real problem, telling *Golf Digest* that he "does not know how to be a proper caddie, and tends to overcelebrate." (To which coach Gary Gilchrist comments, "I would cheer, too, if my daughter sank a putt from 25 feet across the green. Everybody has an opinion until you're in that person's shoes.")

Michelle made it fairly clear what she thought of the incident, saying to reporters, "I've never been so humiliated in my whole life. . . . I can't believe that happened to me in my first Open. I think [Danielle] should apologize." She added, "I was really surprised, because I guess I've always played with really nice people."

The Wies were taken aback by Ammaccapane's treatment of Michelle. "She's young," BJ Wie told the press later. "Danielle is forty, so Michelle is like a daughter. How can she treat a little girl like that? . . . They play golf for a living; they know the etiquette. We don't know; we are still learning." Misunderstanding what Michelle had told him, BJ complained to rules officials that Ammaccapane had pushed Michelle on the fourteenth green, although he later retracted the allegation.

Things got even uglier when the Wies arrived at the clubhouse Saturday morning. Ammaccapane's own father, Ralph, approached the family and had words with BJ, angry at his accusation that Danielle had pushed Michelle. According to BJ, Ralph threatened, "If you continue to lie about my daughter I will take your head off."

"There was no physical contact," BJ explained later. "Michelle talked to the USGA officials to clarify. I think that also maybe I misrepresented what happened."

The incident with Ammaccapane led BJ to recuse himself as caddie, asking Michelle's coach, Gary Gilchrist, to finish out caddying duties on Sunday.

"One thing we tried to explain to BJ was, the less people saw of him, the more people would love his daughter. Not that he's a bad person, but once he stopped caddying and they saw somebody else on the bag, it was easier for everyone to accept her," Gilchrist explained.

"I fired myself because I caused too much trouble out there," BJ later told *Golf Digest*. He admitted that he had made many mistakes as Michelle's caddie, including allowing Michelle to hit out of turn and walking in Danielle's putting line, and expressed regret with the way things turned out. "I am new at this. I caddy for my daughter to save money. If I make mistakes out there, tell me what they are and I will learn."

And that's exactly how Michelle treated it, as a learning experience.

The threesome were matched up together again for Friday's round, which proceeded without any similar incidents. With

Gilchrist carrying her bag on Sunday, Michelle finished the tournament at +14, good enough to tie for thirty-ninth place but far from her goal of shooting four under each day—a goal she later called "ridiculous."

There's no denying that what happened at the Open that year shook Michelle up. BJ later told Eric Adelson of *ESPN: The Magazine,* "Looking back to 2003, mentally both Michelle and I were affected by the incident. Her confidence was down. And the record shows her performance was worse. She struggled with her swing." Only time and more experience allowed Michelle to regain her confidence.

"It's just one of those things she's going to have to get used to," says her old coach Casey Nakama. "You know, some players are a little more picky about movement. It's just a situation where Michelle has to learn the idiosyncrasies of some of the girls."

Not that Michelle didn't have friends on the Tour. Gilchrist noted that several of the women went out of their way to help Michelle feel comfortable, notably Christina Kim, Grace Park, Lorie Kane, and Meg Mallon. "They'd get to know her before judging her and her family," Gilchrist said.

As Christina Kim told *The Honolulu Advertiser* in 2004, "She is so fun-loving. She's fourteen and she doesn't look like it at first and doesn't really act like it, to be honest. Maybe you're asking the wrong person about her—I'm nineteen going on twelve myself—but we get along great. She's funny and very, very intelligent. She has command of her golf game and overall personal well-being. She's an awesome person. Not a little girl, just an awesome person."

And British powerhouse Laura Davies said in interviews,

Golf Etiquette

Just as important as learning the rules of golf is learning golf etiquette—the unwritten rules that outline the behavior expected of golfers. Etiquette on the golf course means being courteous to other players and mindful of your pace of play. Some important points of golf etiquette include:

- While your partner is hitting, stand absolutely still and out of their line of vision. Any motion or noise on your part can distract them and affect their shot.
- The person whose ball is farthest from the hole is always the first person to hit. Play in turn, and be ready to hit your shot as soon as it becomes your turn.
- Tend the flagstick (pull it out of the hole) when your partner is putting. If their ball strikes the flagstick, they get two penalty strokes.
- Try to leave the course in the same condition you found it; rake your bunkers, repair your ball marks, and don't leave scuff marks on the green.
- At the end of the round, shake your partner's hand and congratulate the winner.

At the core of golf etiquette is courtesy and sportsmanship. Treat your partner, as well as the groups in front of and behind you, with the same respect you like to receive. Golf is safest and most enjoyable when everyone follows proper golf etiquette.

"Of course [Michelle] belongs here. Anyone who doesn't believe that has rocks in their heads." During the Weetabix Women's British Open, Davies exclaimed, "Whatever she's doing, it's working at the moment, so she could keep to that. . . . She needs to do what makes her happy."

But when it came to playing against men, even Davies had reservations. "Michelle is a great player," Davies told reporters. "But if I was her I think I'd be more concerned about trying to beat Annika, about trying to be the best women's golfer, before worrying about all that other stuff."

So Michelle was really fighting two battles at once: First, for the right to accept sponsor exemptions and play in LPGA events without having "paid her dues," and second, for the right to follow her dream and compete against men. They're battles she's continuing to fight today.

6

Making It to
the Big Time: 2004

*I feel that if I get afraid of failure,
then I can't go any higher.*

How would you like to earn more than a quarter of a million dollars—but not be allowed to keep it? That's what happened to Michelle during the 2004 golf season. That year, at just fourteen years old, Michelle played in seven LPGA events and one PGA Tour event and finished with two top-ten finishes, including a fourth-place finish at a major. But as an amateur, she couldn't keep the prize money she would have earned—$253,605.

But let's not get ahead of ourselves. Let's go back to the beginning of the season, to the PGA Tour's Sony Open. Michelle had attempted twice before to qualify for the season-opener but failed both times to make it, shooting an 84 in 2000 and a 73 (much better, but still not good enough) in 2002. This time, there was no need to qualify, because her amateur career had caught the attention of a pretty influential person: the governor of Hawaii, Linda Lingle.

After hearing about the ninth-grader's impressive amateur career and goal to play on the PGA Tour, Lingle, along with the Friends of Hawaii Charities, personally requested that Sony invite Hawaii's finest prodigy to their event. Sony was happy to oblige, recognizing that inviting a local star would generate more interest in the tournament.

"I know how hard [the qualifier] can be," Wie admitted as she thanked the sponsors for inviting her. "It's a one-day deal and anything can happen." Sony's decision turned out to be a savvy one. According to *The Honolulu Advertiser,* Michelle Wie's presence at the 2004 Sony Open helped boost attendance by 76 percent from the previous year.

Michelle worked extra hard to prepare, making the trek to Waialae Country Club five times a week for practice rounds. Nine holes after school, three times a week, plus thirty-six holes each weekend, for two months. While most pros play two or three practice rounds getting familiar with a tournament course, Michelle played thirty-five. As Greg Nichols, the director of golf at Ko Olina Golf Club, who's known Michelle since she was eleven years old, told *The Honolulu Advertiser,* "Dreaming is the first step. Then you have to work your tail off to realize that dream. That's what a lot of people don't get. They just see the result. The harder you work, the luckier you get, and she is getting really lucky."

As you read in the Introduction of this book, Michelle's performance at the 2004 Sony Open was heartbreaking—after all that preparation, she ended up shooting 72-68, missing the cut by just one stroke. It was a remarkable performance—good enough to tie U.S. Open champion Jim Furyk and British Open champion Ben Curtis and good enough that her caddie, Bobby Verwey (a former Tour player himself), declared that

Please RSVP . . .

How do you get a special invitation to a professional golf tournament, anyway? Sometimes it's not what you know, it's who you know. For the 2004 Sony Open, it was the governor of Hawaii who stepped in to help get Michelle's exemption. In other tournaments, sponsors haven't needed any special prodding; they recognize on their own that having Michelle Wie in the field will lead to increased fan interest.

These days, Michelle gets so many invites that she has to turn most of them down. As an LPGA nonmember, she is only allowed to accept six sponsor exemptions a year. (But she can play in up to eight events, because two majors, the U.S. Women's Open and the Weetabix Women's British Open, sponsored by the USGA and the Ladies' Golf Union, respectively, are not considered LPGA tournaments.)

Sponsor exemptions have been a tradition in professional tournaments for years. Sponsors—the companies that pay most of the expenses associated with a tournament in exchange for the publicity—generally reserve the right to invite a few players to join the field, players who will help increase ticket sales and local interest in their event.

As PGA Tour vice president Ric Clarson said of Michelle's exemption, "We're in the entertainment business; it's more than just a golf tournament. So when a player like Michelle plays in the Sony Open, it creates national and international attention on, 'Can she do it?' "

she had "the best golf swing I've ever seen in my life." But it wasn't good enough to get her to the weekend rounds. However, she learned important lessons during that tournament that helped carry her through the rest of 2004.

One of those lessons was of the putting variety and was provided by one of Michelle's heroes, PGA Tour player Ernie Els. Els thought that she was accelerating her club on the downswing of her putts and suggested that she use a longer putting stroke, using the same pace throughout. That five-minute lesson paid off, as Michelle three-putted only once throughout the entire tournament. "All because of Ernie Els," Michelle's father later shared with *Golf Digest*. "Michelle is a visual learner, and that's the beauty of her entering PGA Tour events. Because you can learn so much from a player like that."

2004 ON THE LPGA

The year 2004 was a busy one for Michelle. It was the first time she played her full allotment of eight LPGA events—including two majors—without missing a single cut.

She began the season by accepting an invitation to the Safeway International in March. Her final score of two under placed her in a tie for nineteenth place. Not a bad way to start the year.

The Year's First Major: The Kraft Nabisco Championship

Just a week after the Safeway International was the Kraft Nabisco Championship, the first major of the year. In 2003, Michelle had taken ninth place, including a round of 66, which tied for the lowest amateur round in an LPGA major.

This year, playing on another sponsor exemption, she ended at 7-under-par, which was good enough for a fourth-place finish—the best she had done on the LPGA up to now, let alone in a major. The significance of this finish wasn't lost on Michelle, her family, or the gallery.

As Michelle walked up to the eighteenth green on the final day, spectators gave her a standing ovation and some even bowed. Her mother, Bo, burst into tears at the sight.

The first of the LPGA's four majors, the Kraft Nabisco Championship takes place each year in March, at the Mission Hills Country Club in Rancho Mirage, California. This prestigious tournament, originally called the Colgate Dinah Shore (after Dinah Shore, the singer and TV personality who founded it), became the Nabisco Dinah Shore in 1982 and was named a major in 1983. It dropped the "Dinah Shore" in 2000, becoming simply the Nabisco Championship. Then in 2002 it changed names again to the Kraft Nabisco Championship. Through all the changes in its sponsorships and names, however, it has kept its nickname, "the Dinah," and has remained a major.

Go Jump in a Lake!

When many people think of the Kraft Nabisco, they picture the winner taking a running leap into a lake. That's because it's tradition for the winner to do just that—jump into the course's "Champions Lake." Three-time winner Amy Alcott dunked herself in 1988, and the winner has done it ever since.

The 2004 U.S. Women's Open

Michelle played in five other LPGA events in 2004 besides the Kraft Nabisco—including the Michelob Ultra Open, the Evian Masters, the Wendy's Championship for Children, the Samsung World Championship, and the U.S. Women's Open. But it was the U.S. Women's Open in July that held the most significance. It and the Kraft Nabisco were the two majors Michelle played in 2004.

Although Michelle had qualified to play in the U.S. Women's Open the year before, this year she didn't have to, because she was offered a special exemption. Not a sponsor exemption, since the U.S. Women's Open is run by the USGA rather than sponsored by a corporation. Her invitation was unprecedented, as previously no amateurs had gained entry to the tournament in any way other than qualifying.

The decision to invite Wie rather than make her go through the qualifying process was based on her theoretical position on the LPGA's money list. Her play in the previous year would have led to her finishing twenty-eighth on the money list—the top thirty-five on the list automatically get into the tournament.

But some people saw the decision to be preferential treatment, a sellout on the part of the USGA. Ron Sirak, executive editor of *Golf World* magazine, wrote a scathing editorial complaining about the decision: "So what the USGA is saying is that they are giving Wie a reward that goes to professionals without her having to take the risk of turning professional. What's the fairness there? Here's why Wie got a special exemption: It will help TV ratings, give a boost to ticket sales—which are not going to be strong Fourth of July weekend in South

Hadley, Massachusetts—and it will guarantee Wie's presence in other USGA events. Simply put, now she owes them one."

Pointing to Michelle's busy schedule—the Curtis Cup, the U.S. Women's Amateur—Sirak argued that Michelle Wie was getting some "time off from a hectic summer schedule." "Who benefits from this?" Sirak asked. "Wie, and the USGA by guaranteeing her presence in four of their events this year."

Sirak's cynical perspective was mirrored by some of the LPGA players. After all, they had to earn their spots in the tournament; why didn't Michelle have to do the same?

Juli Inkster, a two-time U.S. Women's Open champion, remarked on Michelle's exemptions, "Everybody should earn their way to the Open. It's an experience everybody should go through. You've got to learn how to qualify for things."

"Fair enough," wrote Eric Adelson of *ESPN: The Magazine* in July. "Except not many sports fans out there will be flipping through channels this weekend and remarking, 'Hey, Juli Inkster's on.' And would Juli Inkster, age 14, turn down a chance to play the U.S. Open? Probably not."

But to Michelle's way of thinking, she did earn her way in. When asked during a pretournament press conference whether she felt she was getting special treatment, she said curtly, "I feel like I deserved it because I earned my way here. There's a lot of ways to qualify for this tournament. And one way is to qualify, another way is to get exempt by money ranking, and another way is to get an exemption. And I believe I got exempt because I played in three LPGA tournaments, I got twenty-eighth in the money list, so I would be exempt for this tournament. And that's all I have to say."

WHAT'S SO MAJOR ABOUT MAJORS?

Football has one Superbowl; golf has four. They're called majors, and they're the tournaments that every golfer aspires to win. Why? They have the toughest conditions, the biggest purses, the biggest crowds, the highest-quality fields, and the most storied histories. They're the true measure of greatness: No one can claim to be the best without having won a major. For a professional golfer, they are the ultimate test, and all the other tournaments simply pale in comparison.

Like the PGA, the LPGA offers four majors each year. They are: the Kraft Nabisco, the U.S. Women's Open, the Weetabix Women's British Open, and the McDonald's LPGA Championship. That hasn't always been the case, however. When the LPGA was founded back in 1950, only three tournaments were considered majors: the U.S. Women's Open, plus two others— the Western Open and the Titleholder's Championship. Things have shifted around a bit, as the Western and the Titleholder's went away and others were added.

The most recent addition is, believe it or not, the Weetabix Women's British Open, which became a major in 2001. Whereas the men's British Open (the Open Championship, sponsored by Scotland's Royal and Ancient, golf's oldest governing body) is the oldest championship in golf, dating all the way back to 1860, the women's version didn't become part of the LPGA schedule until 1994. And it is not an official R & A event—rather, it is sponsored by, you guessed it, Weetabix, the cereal manufacturer.

So Michelle—one of a record sixteen teenagers—began the 2004 U.S. Women's Open under a cloud of resentment and added pressure. How did she do? Remember that U.S. Open

courses are set up to be notoriously difficult. The greens run extra fast; the rough
is grown extra long—all to make the experience the ultimate test of skill. Only
the best players score well on a U.S.
Open course.

Whereas the year before Michelle had
begun the Open with an unrealistic goal—
that of shooting 4-under-par each day—this year her goal was
merely to play even par. So the first thing she did was to ask
her dad to carry her bag. She wanted someone familiar with
her game, rather than running the risk of not getting along
with a hired caddie.

Michelle came very close to meeting her goal of even par
on that par-71 course, shooting 71-70-71-73 to end up tied
for thirteenth (with fellow amateur Paula
Creamer). The top twenty receive exemptions for the next year's tournament, so
winning an automatic bid for 2005 was
the best way Michelle knew to silence
her critics.

7

Culture Clash

I'm proud to be Asian-American.
I'm proud that I'm fully Korean,
and that I'm fully American.

By the time she was fifteen years old, Michelle Wie had become something of a household name. She had played in twenty LPGA Tour events, as well as two PGA Tour events, the 2004 and 2005 Sony Opens. Her face had graced the cover of magazines, and tournament organizers everywhere called her with invitations to play in their events. She was becoming one of golf's most recognizable figures, and she was still just a sophomore in high school.

Everyone was amazed by this teenager who could drive the ball farther than professionals twice her age, who hadn't missed an LPGA cut in two years, and who seemed to be able to hang with the big boys.

But what Michelle and her family saw as playing at a high level others saw as pushing a teenaged girl too hard, too soon. Tiger Woods, commentators pointed out, didn't turn pro until he was twenty-one, allowing him to spend two years at college and win twenty amateur events, including the U.S. Amateur title (three times in a row). The sports world buzzed, fretting that teenagers who turn pro too early are more likely to burn out.

The media's fears aren't completely unfounded—look at examples such as tennis phenom Jennifer Capriati, who turned pro at just thirteen years old but found herself arrested a few years later for shoplifting and marijuana possession. The good news is, she did eventually get her life together and has successfully returned to tennis, reaching the World Number 1 ranking in 2001.

Then there's Todd Marinovich, the "Robo-QB," who was famously never allowed to watch cartoons or eat a Big Mac growing up. His father, Marv, a former NFL lineman, literally programmed his son for a life of football, convinced he could create an all-pro. For a while, everything looked good; Todd had a tremendous high school career and led his USC team to the Rose Bowl. In 1991 he got a $2.27 million three-year contract with the L.A. Raiders and became an immediate starter.

But what happened to him? He developed a drug problem and washed out of the NFL after just one year. Since then he's even spent time in jail on drug-related charges. He's never returned to the NFL.

Then, finally, there's Ty Tryon, a golfer who, like Michelle, showed tremendous promise at a young age. "Look out, Tiger Woods," people said as they watched Ty, at age sixteen, become the youngest player ever to make a PGA Tour cut. In December of 2001, at age seventeen, this Leadbetter product became the youngest player ever to turn pro and earn a PGA Tour card, immediately collecting enormous endorsement deals.

But where is he now? Nowhere. All that hype was for naught—after fighting mononucleosis and tonsillitis his rookie year, he got a medical extension for the following year. There he made just four out of twenty-one cuts, finishing 196th on the money list. It wasn't high enough for him to keep his card; he washed out of the PGA Tour and began playing on the Nationwide Tour. But he didn't play well enough to stay on the Nationwide Tour, either. He finished the 2004 season at 199th place, making only six out of twenty-two cuts and earning just $9,058.

IN ALL THREE cases, teens began a professional career before they had the emotional maturity to handle it. And in all three cases, the media assigned blame to the parents for pushing their children too hard.

Critics expressed concern for Michelle's long-term career, worried that her busy schedule would lead her to flame out like Capriati or Tryon. Noting her two missed PGA Tour cuts, *Golf World* magazine ran a piece titled "The Big Queasy," stating: "Over-exposed with a license to impose, Michelle has proven she's more than a Wie bit out of her element."

Part of the problem was the unusual route Michelle's career took. The golf world didn't understand Michelle's decisions. Most golfers follow a traditional path to success: They begin with junior events, playing in the AJGA, earning credits, winning tournaments, building a junior portfolio, and slowly working their way up the ladder of junior events. They focus on winning a college scholarship and gaining more competitive experience there. Or they play the amateur circuit, learning to play against adults. This path has worked just fine for Tiger Woods, Annika Sorenstam, and pretty much all the rest of golf's greats.

Casey Nakama, Michelle's
first coach

Michelle and BJ

Michelle answers
questions from
Ji Yeon Lee of
Korean Golf Digest

PHOTO COURTESY OF
JENNIFER MARIO

Michelle and BJ examine
video clips

PHOTO COURTESY OF PATRICK MICHELETTI

Michelle does a quick
interview with the
Golf Channel

PHOTO COURTESY OF PATRICK MICHELETTI

Michelle arrives for
her appearance on
*The Late Show With
David Letterman.*

Michelle playing in the Sony
Open at Waialae Country Club,
Kahala island of Oahu

Right: Michelle enjoying the game

Michelle speaks to the media
before a big tournament

Michelle spends many hours
on the range perfecting her swing

Michelle putting

Michelle Wie

PHOTO COURTESY OF JENNIFER MARIO

Michelle Wie poses with a trophy

PHOTO COURTESY OF ZUMA PRESS

The Sweet Swing PHOTO COURTESY OF PATRICK MICHELETTI

Wie close up

PHOTO COURTESY OF PATRICK MICHELETTI

Wie lines up a putt

PHOTO COURTESY OF PATRICK MICHELETT

Wie with parents watching

PHOTO COURTESY OF PATRICK MICHELETTI

Wie playing in a tournament
at Pearl County Club island of Oahu

Michelle did things a little differently; at age twelve she had already played in LPGA events. At fourteen, she was invited to play in the PGA Tour's Sony Open. She never joined the AJGA, and she stopped playing against juniors altogether by the time she was fifteen. She basically skipped straight from children's events in Hawaii to accepting sponsor exemptions on the PGA Tour.

But Michelle and her family had a reason for this. Living in Hawaii was the main problem; traveling back and forth to junior tournaments on the mainland would have strained the family's budget. Michelle's parents earned a comfortable living, but even so they couldn't afford to send Michelle to every junior or amateur event. Air travel for three, hotel costs, tournament fees, not to mention Michelle's missing more school than most players, forced the Wies to pick and choose their tournaments carefully. And when one is looking at the way the Wies have handled Michelle's career, there's another factor to consider as well.

A PRODUCT OF TWO WORLDS

The media, in looking for something to criticize in Michelle's success story, has missed an important point: While they worry that Michelle is being pushed too hard, they forget that Michelle is not your typical teenager; she comes from a different cultural background.

As a Korean-American, Michelle was raised with elements of both American and Korean cultures. The American part of her goes to the movies with her friends, chats online and sends text messages on her cell phone, watches cartoons, and laughs at Jim Carrey in *Dumb & Dumber*.

The Korean side of her rises early to hit balls until dark, plays nine holes every day after school, works out at the gym four days a week, and doesn't leave the range until she has perfected every new skill her coaches teach her. When it's time to go to sleep, she doesn't tell her parents "good night"; she says, "anyonghi choomoosayo."

But the American media, looking at her from a purely American perspective, see what many Americans do—a Capriati or Marinovich pushed hard by their parents—and think that this can only lead to problems down the road.

"We've seen what happened to other sports that were invaded by teen angels, namely women's tennis, gymnastics, and the NBA," wrote *The Washington Post* columnist Sally Jenkins. "How long before golf is populated by uneducated flameouts who buckle and warp under the workload, the pressure of expectations, white hot lights and overbearing stage parents?"

But remember the high-schoolers' schedule in Korea? They work constantly, attending school until 4:00 P.M., practicing a sport or going to an after-school tutoring program until dark, then doing homework late into the night. If they're caught up on their work, it's time for more work: foreign language study, college entrance exam preparation, more practice.

Put simply, Korean parents expect more from their children. They believe anything less would be poor parenting. But with those high expectations comes support. It's the kids' jobs to do well in school; it's the parents' jobs to do everything they can to help their kids do well in school.

With this attitude firmly entrenched from such an early age, kids, eventually, expect more from themselves. It's one of the reasons why the South Korean literacy rate hovers at around 98 percent, why Korea consistently ranks in the top ten at winning Olympic medals although it ranks twenty-fourth in terms of population, and why LPGA leaderboards tend to be dominated by Korean women. The Korean media doesn't stress over whether or not children are having enough of a childhood—putting in the effort is the cultural norm, the one both BJ and Bo grew up with.

That's not to say BJ and Bo are hard on Michelle. In fact, as Casey Nakama points out, they never give her a hard time on the golf course. During the three years he worked with her, he saw her nearly every day. Not once, he says, did he see them scold her. "I never saw that," he says. "Ever. And they were here a lot! Both parents would be here. The last thing in the world kids need is to think that if they play poorly they're going to get yelled at. The last thing they need is to feel like they're disappointing their parents. That's something I give BJ credit for—they've never, ever been down on her."

Perhaps most important of all, golf doesn't make Michelle feel pressured; in fact, it does the opposite. Asked about pressure at a press conference, she said, "When I play golf I actually feel unstressed. After all my exams I go out on the range and hit tons and tons of balls. . . . I was talking to my sports psychologist and he was like, 'Is there any problem you need to talk about on the golf course?' I was like, 'No, I have to talk about my math tests.'"

Her parents provide not pressure but support. As Nakama puts it, "A kid will only get as good as their parents can sacrifice." Being an only child has helped; if she had sisters or brothers, her parents would have to divide their time among all their children. As it is, she gets their undivided attention. Their attendance at all of her practices, their support for her at all of her tournaments, make her feel, as her coach Gary Gilchrist puts it, "fully secure and loved." "Her family values are so strong," he says. "They have such a good plan and are committed to the plan."

Michelle, as a Korean-American, straddles two cultures. So far, she has been able to take elements from both and use that combination to her advantage—working long hours to perfect her game while still enjoying fun, freedom, and time with friends. She has something that was missing from the lives of young Capriati, Marinovich, or Tryon—a healthy balance between focus and fun.

As Gary Gilchrist points out, Michelle has other things in her life besides golf. "If you took golf away from her, she wouldn't feel inadequate," he says. "She knows she's good at school, she knows she's good at public speaking, she knows she's a little clumsy, and she's okay with it. She knows she loves to shop, to design earrings. She doesn't get her whole identity out of being a great player. She's well-rounded."

MEANWHILE, AS MICHELLE told Eric Adelson of *ESPN: The Magazine,* she enjoys aiming high and working hard. "I'm proud to be Asian-American," she said. "I'm proud that I'm fully Korean, and that I'm fully American. I want to represent hope, the belief that it can happen. I made my goals very high, and it's going to be very hard for me. But I enjoy it."

So which side will win out? Will she crack under the pressure of doing so much at such a young age? Or will her Korean work ethic, combined with her American opportunities, create something altogether new?

Only time will tell. But since she is currently one of the world's best-paid female athletes, it would be hard to argue that it's not working for her. Michelle said it best when she told *Golf for Women* magazine, "I think before you criticize someone you should get to know them. The thing that makes me really mad is when people compare me to the young tennis stars who burned out. They're assuming the same thing for me. But they don't know me. I think my parents are doing a good job. If it looks like I'll grow up and wear a nose ring or do drugs, then I guess they can make a judgment. But I'm not doing any of those things now."

8

Big Dreams,
Big Results: 2005

Dream big and I will reach the
sky; dream small and my feet will
never get off the ground.

If 2004 was a big year for Michelle, 2005 was the biggest yet. Now a tenth-grader at the Punahou School, she played in eight LPGA events, including all four majors, plus two PGA Tour events. But there was one goal she was hungry to accomplish; that was her dream to someday play in the Masters. In 2005, she got closer to realizing that dream than she ever had.

Her golf season began at the Sony Open in January, the same PGA Tour tournament where, the year before, she had come so close to making the cut—missing by just one stroke.

She finished day 1 with a 75, making only one birdie the whole round. "After missing the cut by one last year, I think I took for granted that I was going to play better. Last year, everything went too easily," she said afterward.

Day 2 was no better. She had to score 67 in order to make the cut but saw that goal disappear by the sixth hole. First, she missed the fairway of the par 4, hitting into the right rough behind some palm trees. Then, trying to hit past the trees back into the fairway, she came up short. She hit a wedge with her third shot but still didn't make it onto the green. Her fourth shot finally made it to the green but rolled 8 feet past the hole.

At this point she had an 8-foot putt to make a bogey, not the greatest result but nothing she couldn't recover from. But she failed to make the putt and instead three-putted from there to take a shocking triple-bogey 7. Ouch.

She ended up missing the Sony Open cut by seven strokes this time around at 9-over-par, a disappointment after coming so close the year before. But she tried to stay positive. "I learned a lot of things this week, more than last year, I think," she said afterward. "I think when you play bad, you learn a lot more."

MICHELLE HAD A chance to begin applying what she learned at the SBS Open, the LPGA's first full-field event of the year, held annually at the Turtle Bay Resort on her home island of Oahu. She scored three seventies during the three-round tournament, for a total of 6-under-par—good enough to tie for second along with the LPGA's top American, Cristie Kerr, a six-time champion. Michelle and Kerr were just two strokes off the winner, Jennifer Rosales.

Rosales may have won the tournament, but Michelle was the only player in the field who shot all three rounds under par. A couple of three-putts were the only thing blocking her way to a victory. Admittedly nervous before the tournament began, she ended up proud of her performance, saying in a posttournament press conference that her finish—since it was

What's So Bad About a Three-Putt?

Pars depend on a player taking just two putts once they've reached the green. One-putts are ideal, of course, but not always realistic. That's why golfers get so frustrated when they three-putt. Three-putts mean bogeys or worse, erase leads, and can ruin a round and a tournament.

her best to date, and happened in her home state of Hawaii—felt like a win.

Playing on sponsor exemptions, Michelle spent her spring break competing first in the Safeway International, where she finished tied for twelfth, then in the Kraft Nabisco, her first major of the year. She had played this tournament twice before, finishing ninth in 2003 and fourth in 2004. This year, although she was determined to beat or at least match her previous years' performances, things didn't go quite as well, and she finished in a tie for fourteenth.

After the school year ended in early June, she had even more time to focus on golf and spent her days at Ko Olina Golf Club, practicing hard for the five tournaments she would play over the summer.

First up, in June, came the McDonald's LPGA Championship in Havre de Grace, Maryland. Once again, her sponsor exemptions raised a great hue and cry. No amateur had received a sponsor exemption for the tournament in its fifty-one-year history, and many people felt that the LPGA Championship should be reserved for, well, the LPGA.

In fact, the LPGA itself hadn't been so sure about granting

Michelle the exemption. But McDonald's, the main corporate sponsor of the event, drove a hard bargain: Allow us to put an amateur in the field, or we'll drop our sponsorship of the tournament. "The people at McDonald's were very, very, very, very insistent," a source told *Golf World* magazine. "They were upset that they were the only major not to have Wie." In the end they got their way, of course, and added Michelle to the field as well as five other players of their choosing.

Cristie Kerr, the LPGA's top American, who had tied for second with Michelle at the SBS Open earlier in the year, complained to *Sports Illustrated* magazine, "This is the kind of tournament you should earn your way into. If we have to resort to this sort of thing for publicity, maybe we should look at other ways."

Asked afterward if she felt extra pressure due to this resentment, Michelle responded simply, "Not really. I'm pretty used to people not wanting me at tournaments by now. It didn't really give me that feeling of: oh, I have to prove it to them. I don't want to prove anything to anyone. I was really happy to be here and I felt like I finished really strong."

And finish strong she did. She showed she belonged with another second-place finish, just three strokes behind winner Annika Sorenstam—Michelle's best finish to date in an LPGA major. Cristie Kerr, meanwhile, tied for thirty-third.

"Finishing second to Annika Sorenstam, and only by three strokes, is like winning these days on the LPGA Tour," wrote Bill Kwon of *The Honolulu Advertiser.* Why? Because Annika Sorenstam is the most dominant player in women's golf. At the time of the LPGA Championship, Annika was on a roll. She had won sixty-one tournaments, including five of her last seven, and her goal for the year was to win all four majors, an accomplishment that is called the "Grand Slam" of golf.

Tell Me More About Annika Sorenstam . . .

If Michelle plans to become the number-one player on the LPGA, she has her work cut out for her. Because right now that spot is occupied by Annika Sorenstam, one of the most dominant female golfers of all time. She's the LPGA's version of Tiger Woods.

Already a member of the LPGA's Hall of Fame at just thirty-five years old, the eight-time Player of the Year has won 67 tournaments as of this writing, including nine majors, with more surely on the way. Since 2000, she's won at least five tournaments a year, and she has career earnings of more than $18 million—$7 million more than the next-highest player, Karrie Webb!

Originally from Stockholm, Sweden, Annika moved to the United States at age nineteen, played at the University of Arizona to gain experience, and then began her systematic destruction of LPGA records. In 2005, her eleventh year on tour, she played in twenty tournaments and won ten of them—a staggering 50 percent win rate. Even Tiger doesn't match it—during his best year to date (2001), he won six of the twenty-three tournaments entered—"just" 26 percent.

Back when the LPGA offered only three majors—the U.S. Open, the Titleholder's, and the Western Open—Babe Didrikson Zaharias won all three. And in 1974, a year the LPGA offered only two majors (the Women's U.S. Open and the LPGA Championship), Sandra Haynie captured both titles. But no woman has ever swept all four majors, and Annika had decided this was her year to step up and get it done. She had made good on her goal thus far, winning the Kraft Nabisco by eight strokes over second-placer Rosie Jones. Now Annika was halfway to her goal, winning by three over Michelle at the McDonald's LPGA Championship.

"You are witnessing one of the greatest runs of any athlete in any sport at any time," LPGA Tour commissioner Ty Votaw said of Annika's quest.

No one has ever won what we think of as the modern Grand Slam on the PGA Tour, either, although Tiger Woods won his own version of one, the "Tiger Slam," during the 2000–2001 seasons, when he won four consecutive majors, just not all in the same calendar year.

Back in 1930, when PGA majors consisted of the British Open, the British Amateur, the U.S. Open, and the U.S. Amateur championships, amateur Bobby Jones swept all four. They didn't actually have a name for it yet, though some writers referred to it as the "Impregnable Quadrilateral." Eventually, O.B. Keeler, a writer for *The Atlanta Journal,* borrowed a bridge term to coin the phrase "Grand Slam." Meanwhile, the modern Grand Slam continues to elude both men and women.

JUST TWO WEEKS after the McDonald's LPGA Championship came the U.S. Women's Open, played at Cherry Hills Country Club in Cherry Hills Village, Colorado. This time, Michelle had earned her way in with her T13 (tie for thirteenth) finish the year before. (Everyone who places in the top twenty gets an automatic bid the following year.)

Michelle's first three rounds were nothing short of remarkable. She shot 69-73-72 to end up with a share of the lead going into Sunday's round. Another 73 would have won the tournament for her. Instead, she ended up with an 82—a score she hadn't posted in competition in years. She opened with a double bogey, and her round never picked up from there. She had a chance to regain some momentum on number 7, a short par 4. Michelle hit a beautiful approach shot and had just a 2-foot putt for birdie. "Oh my gosh," she gasped, with a hand over her mouth, when the ball lipped out.

"'Difficult' would be too easy a word," Michelle told the press afterward. "It was really hard out there for me today."

Another player was just as disappointed as Michelle, if not more so: Annika Sorenstam. She had just as bad a day and tied with Michelle for twenty-third place.

The tournament was won with an unlikely shot by an unknown named Birdie Kim. The South Korean holed a bunker shot on 18 for a miracle birdie that unseated Morgan Pressel and Brittany Lang, two teenaged amateurs who ended up tying for second place. And Annika would have to wait another year before trying for the Grand Slam again. Losing the Women's Open to Birdie Kim meant the end of that dream for 2005.

To be fair, the U.S. Women's Open has a long history of unseating leaders on the final day. Michelle and Annika were in good company, plunging from their spots on top of the leaderboard to end up tied for twenty-third. Back in 1990, Patty Sheehan began the final round of the U.S. Women's Open with a nine-stroke lead, only to lose to Betsy King. (Sheehan went on to be a two-time winner, though, in 1992 and 1994.) In 1994, Helen Alfredsson had a seven-stroke lead but finished eight shots back of winner Sheehan.

And it's not just women who can be affected this way. PGA Tour professional Retief Goosen, a South African who's won two tournaments on the PGA Tour, began the final day at the 2005 U.S. Open with a large enough lead that people figured his last round was merely a formality. But what happened? Both he and his playing partner that day, Jason Gore, a Nationwide Tour player who had also wowed the crowds, blew up. Goosen shot an 81, and Gore shot an 84. What could have been first- and second-place finishes ended up being ties for eleventh and forty-ninth. The same thing happened to Michelle's hero, Ernie Els, another two-time PGA Tour champion, in 2004. Beginning the final day in the lead, he shot an 80 on Sunday to see the title slip from his fingers. At the U.S. Open, literally anything can happen.

LIFE ON THE PGA TOUR

The Sony Open wasn't the only PGA Tour event that Michelle played in 2005. In July, she also played in the John Deere Classic, held in Silvis, Illinois.

She accepted the invitation for this event for several reasons: For one thing, the winner of the tournament receives an automatic invitation to play in the men's British Open—the Open Championship—a tournament she dreamed of one day playing. For another, because of its timing—a week before the Open Championship—many of the PGA Tour's top players would be elsewhere. This meant she would have an excellent chance of making the cut. And last, as she said to the press, she wanted as many chances as possible to play against the men. "The more PGA Tour events I play, the better my chance of making the cut and eventually becoming the first female member on the PGA Tour," she said. "When I go out and play in a PGA Tour event, I don't go there to win now but to learn from the best."

Mark Hensby, the Australian defending champion of the John Deere, caused a stir when he admonished the Wie family for allowing her to play in the tournament. It started when he entered the media tent for preround interviews right after Michelle had finished hers and discovered that he would be talking to an empty room—when Michelle had left, so had the press. It was a real check to his ego.

"I don't think a fifteen-year-old girl who's done nothing at all should get a sponsor's invitation to a PGA Tour event," he complained. "But I don't blame the John Deere Classic or Michelle. I blame her parents, and the people running her affairs. Michelle should be playing against girls her own age. She's obviously a very good player, but she's only ever won one junior tournament." (Apparently he was unaware that the U.S. Women's Amateur Public Links, which she had won two years earlier, was an adults' event.)

This wasn't Michelle's first time running across Hensby. They had met in 2003 at the Boise Open, a Nationwide Tour event. He had shared his feelings about her then, too. "Women's golf and men's golf are two different things, and I don't understand what they're all trying to prove," Hensby said to reporters at the time. "The bottom line is Michelle shouldn't be playing with us. It's as simple as that. She should be at school, man. There's plenty of time for her to play golf, and now's definitely not the time to play with us. I don't know what her parents are thinking throwing her into an arena like this." Apparently not much had changed in two years.

Despite Hensby's comments this go-around, Michelle finished her first round with a score of 1-under-par. On day 2, wearing a belt with a sparkly "68" on the buckle, Michelle was ready to score low and make the cut. She couldn't have asked to do any better than she did in her first nine holes, where she made four birdies and just one bogey to make the turn at three under.

But things took a turn for the worse on her very last four holes. Spotting a leaderboard on the fifteenth hole, she noticed that Mark Hensby was just two strokes ahead. Still three under, she pulled out a 3 wood instead of a more conservative 5 wood, looking to birdie the hole. But her drive landed in a bunker. That resulted in a double bogey, which she followed up with another bogey—thereby erasing those three strokes and ending up even par for the round. Had she simply played those last four holes at even par, she likely would have made the cut. As it was, she missed by two strokes.

Even though Michelle didn't make the cut, the tournament itself still benefited quite a bit by her presence. According to *The Honolulu Advertiser,* tournament organizers had to add a second media tent just to handle the influx. Officials expected attendance to increase by 10 percent with Michelle in the field; instead, the tournament saw an increase of 40 percent, to $2.8 million, according to *Fortune* magazine. TV viewership went up 54 percent from the year before, and at the end of the day, the tournament ended up raising $1 million more for charity than it had the year before.

STANDING HER GROUND

It wasn't just Mark Hensby wondering if Michelle's family was making the right choice, allowing her to play against men. Critics in the press wondered the same thing.

Some detractors went so far as to claim that while Michelle's dream to play against men might help Michelle, it would somehow hurt women's golf.

Frank Deford, one of *Sports Illustrated*'s most respected writers, wrote a column in which he argued that Michelle should "play against her own kind."

"You may beat most men on the golf course, but every time you try that, you're beating women's sports more than you're beating men golfers," he wrote.

According to Deford, Michelle's dream of playing against men would damage women's sports irreparably. "She is, obviously, an absolute marvel—so good, in fact, that everybody is watching her, and if, during her long, magnificent career that lies ahead, she spends her time chasing pie in the sky and men in spikes, she will only, ultimately and primarily, detract from women's golf and, really, all of women's sport."

But Michelle was determined to follow her own path. Soon after accepting her exemption to the John Deere Classic (and earning howls from many in the golf community), she wrote an impassioned letter to the Associated Press explaining her choices. Here's what it said:

This is Michelle Wie. I would like to take this opportunity to clarify myself with regards to playing in professional events and not following the conventional path that many great golfers have gone through.

I wanted to play in the AJGA national junior golf tournaments, but I wasn't allowed to play. I was too young. The AJGA has an age restriction. Not many people know about it. Since I wasn't allowed to play in the AJGA, I played in local junior events. I started dominating when I was 9–10 years old. So I started to play in the 15–17 age groups. I again dominated there so I started playing local women's events. I started dominating again. I won the local women's professional event by 13 strokes. Since there were only three women's events in Hawaii, I started to play in men's events. Once I started playing in men's events, I started to love them. Then I started playing in LPGA events at age 12. I wasn't given an exemption into the LPGA tournament; I made it through Monday qualifying. I wasn't given anything. And that year, I qualified for another LPGA event. So I worked my way up.

By the time I was allowed to play in AJGA tournaments at age 13, I already made the top 10 at an LPGA major and won an adult USGA amateur tournament. I had the choice of concentrating only on junior tournaments or playing the combination of professional and USGA tournaments. I chose the latter. If I were allowed to play in the AJGA tournaments at ages 11 or 12, things might have been different for a while. But I think I would have come back to the same choice.

As a matter of fact, traveling to an AJGA tournament costs the same as traveling to an LPGA tournament. If a Bentley and a Toyota cost the same, wouldn't anyone get a Bentley? I got a Bentley and do not regret my decision.

People always ask why I do what I do and why not just follow the conventional path. My answer is very simple. I always wanted to push myself to the limit. I started walking when I was nine months old and I started reading when I was just over one year old. I started playing golf when I was 4 and shot a 64 when I was 10. I was not only a girl on the boys' baseball team but also the best hitter. I qualified for the WAPL when I was 10 years old and made the cut. I always *wanted to do things fast. I always wanted to be the first and youngest to do things.*

I feel grateful for all the sponsor exemptions that the tournaments have offered to me. I cherish each and every one of them. When I play in a pro event, whether it is an LPGA or PGA event, I feel privileged to play because I get to meet and get to know all the players. This is my fourth year playing on the LPGA tour. I now feel comfortable with the players and the tour itself. When I first came out on the tour, I felt lost and confused. I didn't know what to expect. But as I played more events, the tour felt more and more like home. I guess another reason I am playing professional events is to gain as much experience as I can before I turn pro. A lot of rookies don't do their best because they experience the same thing as I experienced in the first year, "lost and confused." Junior tournaments and pro tournaments are very different. The atmosphere and course set-up are completely different.

A lot of people criticize my choice to play in the PGA Tour events, but I am really happy to be there. I get to know the players and get to play a PGA Tour course. It's really fun and I think it helps me to get ready for my ultimate goal of becoming a PGA Tour member. I am not afraid of failure, and I can not be. When I went to the Great Wall of China, I was really excited. I was walking up the stairs and going really high. I got tired and I looked down. At that point I saw how high I was and what would happen if I fell. I collapsed right at that very moment and sat down on the steps. I refused to go another step higher and crawled my way down. I feel that if I get afraid of failure, then I can't go any higher. Now I regret that I did not walk up higher to see what is up there.

A lot of the critics say that I should win more junior girls' tournaments to boost my confidence and that missing cuts in PGA events will ruin my confidence. I don't believe in that statement. I believe that failure is the greatest thing that happens to my golf game. It helps me recognize my mistakes. For example, when I play a bad shot in a tournament and it turns out good, then I don't think about it and then I would play that shot again. But if it turns out bad, I recognize that I hit a bad shot and will never play it again. When I go out and play in a PGA Tour event, I don't go there to win now, but to learn from the best. I missed the cut in my first three LPGA tournaments. The more PGA events I play, the better chance I make the cut and eventually win. I am grateful for every exemption and I cherish all of them. If someone gave you a 13-carat diamond ring, wouldn't you accept it? That is what I think the PGA exemptions are—13-carat diamond rings.

I am not going to do whatever the critics want me to do because they always change their minds anyway. No matter what the critics say about me, I am going to do whatever my heart tells me to do and I thank my parents for always backing me up. Dream big and I will reach the sky; dream small and my feet will never get off the ground.

COMING CLOSE TO A DREAM

But 2005 was a big year for Michelle for another reason: It was the best chance to date of achieving her goal of one day playing in the Masters. That's no small goal—the Masters, one of the PGA Tour's four majors—is normally reserved for only the top players in the world, either previous champions of PGA and USGA events or top Tour money winners. Not just anyone gets an invitation for the Masters.

It was highly unlikely that Michelle would win any PGA Tour events and impossible that she would place high on the money list, so she focused on entering through the back door—the U.S. Amateur Public Links (the men's version of the U.S. Women's Amateur Publinx, the tournament she had won in 2003). The winner of the men's Publinx receives an automatic invitation to the Masters, and Michelle saw this as her best opportunity to get into the prestigious event.

Normally an all-male event, the U.S. Amateur Publinx is held each year in July. To enter, each player must go through several qualifying rounds; only those who qualify are allowed to play in the tournament itself. Following qualifiers, the tournament then has two parts, just like in the Women's Amateur Publinx (described in chapter 4): First, there are two days of stroke play. At the end of the two days, the field is cut in half; those who make the cut proceed to match play rounds, and those who don't go home early.

In order to qualify, Michelle beat out eighty-three other amateurs, all men, to win her spot in the actual tournament. She managed to do just that with style, placing first to win medalist honors in her qualifying tournament. During the stroke play of the actual tournament, Michelle struggled a bit but managed to make the cut.

Match play consisted of six rounds, with sixty-four players competing for the title. Michelle won her first match handily, beating twenty-three-year-old Will Claxton by the sixteenth hole. She went on to win her next two matches, 6 and 5 over CD Hockersmith and 3 and 1 over Jim Renner.

This took her all the way to the quarterfinals—only eight

players made it that far. But she lost her fourth and final match 5 and 4 to Clay Ogden, a twenty-year-old junior at Brigham Young University, who went on to win the tournament.

Once again, her presence in a men's event rankled some of the other players. This time it was a forty-five-year-old golfer named Danny Green, the oldest amateur in the field. "Personally, I don't think she should be here, but that's just my opinion," Green said to the press. "I think she should play in women's tournaments because they don't let men play in the women's tournaments. . . . I think I know what she's aspiring to do, but I think she would be a better player in the long run if she plays where she could win and build up more confidence. I mean, if she plays in the men's ranks and never wins, I don't think that's good for her long-term goals."

Michelle wasn't bothered by Green's attitude. When asked about his comments, she responded frankly, "I don't care what [people] think or say. I qualified to be here and I feel I earned my spot."

Although Michelle didn't achieve her dream of winning the tournament and receiving that Masters bid, she came closer than any other fifteen-year-old and certainly any other female had ever come. When most people heard of the teenager's desire to play in the Masters, they laughed. After the U.S. Amateur Publinx, no one was laughing.

A LONG SUMMER

Michelle didn't take a break after the Publinx—she moved right along to Evian-les-Bains, France, to play in the Evian Masters, her fourth tournament in as many weeks. Many people consider the Evian Masters to be the LPGA's "fifth major" because of its large purse—$2.5 million, the second-largest purse of any LPGA event.

Michelle hit only two fairways in the first round, ending with a 3-over-par 75. "Playing like this isn't really fun," she said afterward, "but there's nothing else I'd rather be doing." Determining that part of the problem was her caddie, Brian Smallwood, whom the Wies had hired for the event, Michelle let him go and put her father back on her bag.

But her father wasn't a perfect replacement: During the third round, BJ gave Michelle the wrong yardage on the fourth hole—30 yards wrong. "It was 116 yards, and I gave her 146," he later told *Golf Today,* laughing. "The ball flew over the green and she made triple bogey. She's still blaming me for that."

Nonetheless, with her father on the bag Michelle proceeded to shoot three consecutive under-par rounds (70, 68, and 68) to finish tied for second along with Mexican player Lorena Ochoa. Paula Creamer, a teenaged rookie, left everyone behind, winning by eight strokes.

And still Michelle's summer wasn't over. She had one more tournament to play before returning to school: the Weetabix Women's British Open, the fourth and final major of the year.

This would be Michelle's first appearance in the event. Though she had wanted to play in years prior, it was only in 2005 that the Ladies' Golf Union—the organizers of the European event—extended the field to include amateurs and gave her an invitation. "We have followed Michelle's development over the last two years with great interest and admiration and in particular her performance in major championships," LGU chief executive Andy Salmon said in a statement.

Like she did at the Evian Masters, Michelle opened with a disappointing 75, 3-over-par. She wasn't the only player struggling, though. It was unseasonably cold for July, with plenty of nasty wind and rain thrown in. "I've played in rain before. I've played in the wind before. I played when it was cold before. But all put together was really hectic," said Wie in a postround interview. "It's the first time I played in the British Open and I felt like I got the whole package."

Conditions improved over the next few days, and Michelle shot 67, 67, and 69 to end the tournament at ten under, good enough for a tie for third place. That would've been worth $142,000, had she been allowed to keep the money.

The year 2005 was one about which Michelle really couldn't complain. She played in three men's and eight LPGA events and had four top-five finishes, including two in majors. Contrast that with Annika Sorenstam. Before turning pro, Annika played in only four LPGA events and her best finish was a fourth-place spot at the Standard Register PING. Michelle had plenty of reasons to be satisfied with her year so far.

All in all, Michelle ended the summer earning more than $680,000, although as an amateur she didn't keep a penny. Her next tournament—the Samsung World Championship—was in October. And by then, things would have changed. Michelle was about to turn pro.

9

Going Pro

I'm ready.

THE BIG ANNOUNCEMENT

The applause finally died as the girl in a bright pink Nike shirt and curled hair, perched high on a director's chair onstage at the front of the room, took the microphone. Everyone strained to get a good view as Michelle Wie, still six days away from turning sixteen, started to speak softly.

"I just want to thank everyone for coming today; I know it's not that easy to come to Hawaii," she began. "And I want to thank everyone for spending this special day with me. I'm finally happy to say that I'm a pro as of today.

"The first time I grabbed a golf club, I knew I'd do it for the rest of my life and I loved it. Some twelve years later, I'm finally turning pro, and I'm so excited. I'm really happy to join the Nike and the Sony family, and I'm so grateful for all the opportunities they gave me, and all the flexibility they gave me. They understand that my first priority is school. I know I'm going to graduate high school, and hopefully achieve my goal of graduating college. More than ever before I'm just going to practice harder than ever to try and become the best golfer in the world."

It was October 5, 2005, and with her father snapping photos from the front row, Michelle had just made the biggest announcement of her golf career: She was now a professional. Until now, no matter how well she placed in a big tournament, she wasn't playing for the money but for the experience. Now things were changing.

As her father said after Michelle's press conference, "Becoming a professional means she will have more responsibility. She has to be able to handle much higher expectations. She'll have extra pressure."

Extra pressure, yes. And extra money, too. Michelle's parents had been helping Michelle plan this day for several months now and had already lined up sponsorships worth millions. On October 5, Michelle became the highest-paid female golfer on the planet. And she still didn't even have a driver's license.

SPONSORSHIPS

Professional athletes make money several different ways—they can earn it through tournament winnings and appearance fees, of course, but the big money is in sponsorships.

Why do you think Michelle was wearing that bright pink shirt with the familiar swoosh? It was no secret that Michelle favored Nike products. And now that she was a pro, she could turn something as simple as her choice of golfwear into a moneymaking endeavor.

Nike, with that swoosh logo, was now Michelle's biggest sponsor. With the help of Michelle's agent, Ross Berlin of the William Morris Agency, Michelle's parents arranged deals with several huge companies, including Nike and Sony, which would pay her for endorsing their products.

What exactly is a sponsorship? For some professional athletes, sponsorships are where they make the majority of their earnings. Tiger Woods, for example, earned $9.9 million in 2005 playing golf but six times that—$60 million—from his sponsorships with Nike and Buick!

Annika Sorenstam, who was the highest-paid female golfer in the world until Michelle came along, earns about $6 million each year from her sponsorships with Callaway Golf, Mercedes-Benz, Oakley, Cutter & Buck, Rolex, Kraft, and ADT. All that money plus free clubs, cars, sunglasses, golfwear, watches, and mac and cheese!

So when you see a golfer with "TaylorMade" on his hat, "PING" on his shirt, and "Titleist" on his golf bag, realize that each one of those logo placements is costing that company money, and putting money in the golfer's pocket. Even caddies get paid for the brands of clothing they wear on the course— rates go up depending on how likely the caddie is to appear on television.

But not just anyone gets such sweet deals. You have to have a big name to get big sponsorships, because the sponsors aren't in it just to be nice—they're in it to make money. They know that if a big-name player is using their products, then other people will want to use those products, too. For the sponsors, it's an investment; and in this case, they're investing in Michelle.

For most sponsors, it's critical to match the athlete with the product. With Nike, it's an obvious choice: Michelle likes wearing Nike clothing and plays with Nike clubs.

With Sony, it was a little more complicated. No one wears Sony clothes or plays golf with Sony clubs. But Sony was, after all, the company that had given Michelle one of her most critical exemptions: the exemption to the 2004 Sony Open, her first foray onto the PGA Tour. For Sony, it was about capitalizing on Michelle's innovation and style.

"It was interesting how quickly this came together for us because we weren't in the market for an athlete," Mike Fasulo, chief marketing officer for Sony, told the press. "But we'd had a long-term relationship already with Michelle and when she contemplated turning pro, it just started to roll for both parties."

It wasn't that long ago that such enormous sponsorships were unheard of or were based purely on years of proven performance. Arnold Palmer, one of golf's greatest legends, for example, didn't hire an agent until 1960, after he'd already won the Masters, and he famously never signed an actual contract; it was a "handshake agreement." That handshake agreement, by the way, was with Mark McCormack, founder of IMG, the sports agency that now represents both Tiger Woods and Annika Sorenstam.

But television has changed the sports world. Sponsors realize that golfers can act essentially as walking billboards, and they're willing to pay quite a bit for that advertising space. Now when a hot new athlete comes down the pike, companies jockey for the chance to blaze their logo on that athlete's chest, whether the athlete has proved himself or not.

When Tiger Woods turned pro, back in 1996, he set a new record: He signed a five-year deal with Nike worth $40 million before he'd even won a single tournament as a profes-

Pop Quiz

What do Michelle Wie, Clint Eastwood, and John Travolta have in common? They all hired the William Morris Agency to handle their deals and negotiations. So how did Michelle choose William Morris, a company associated more with Hollywood than with the sports world?

Michelle says it's *because* they have no other golfers on their client list. "I'm an only child, so I guess I'm used to being exclusive," she explained to *Fortune* magazine.

sional. Many wondered whether a golfer, let alone a rookie golfer, was worth that kind of money. Like it has with Michelle, it led to a certain amount of jealousy among the ranks. PGA Tour players thought it was a mistake to throw that kind of money at a rookie who hadn't yet won anything on tour. Others simply grew tired of all the hype; at every interview, every press conference, players would be questioned not about their own game but about how they felt about Tiger.

"Some guys gave me the cold shoulder," Woods said later. "Some guys wouldn't talk to me at all."

But soon players came to realize how Tiger's moneymaking abilities could help them. When Tiger Woods won the 1997 Masters, the Sunday TV ratings ran a record 14.1—the highest ratings that a golf tournament had ever received. One month later, a new TV contract increased PGA Tour purses by 40 percent. And now, ten years later, prize money on the Tour has tripled.

Carolyn Bivens, commissioner of the LPGA Tour, held a meeting with LPGA players soon after Michelle turned pro, asking them to look at the big picture. "It's a rising tide that lifts all the boats," she said. "Michelle is good for golf just as Tiger was good for golf. There are a lot of people who may not follow golf otherwise but tune in when you've got a Michelle or a Tiger out there."

GIVING BACK

As she sat on the stage, Michelle continued to talk about her new position, considering how she could make a difference in the world: "Turning pro has a lot of benefits. Finally I'm so grateful to be in a position to help people," she said. "Over the last month, so many people have lost so many things, and it's been really heart wrenching. As an American citizen, I felt like it was my duty to donate $500,000 to Hurricane Katrina. Every single cent will go to the people."

Six weeks earlier, Hurricane Katrina had devastated the

A Note About Appearance Fees

When golfers charge money simply for playing in a tournament, those earnings are called "appearance fees." The PGA and the LPGA tours forbid players from collecting appearance fees for their events, but appearance fees are allowed for most overseas events. The more popular a player is, the more they can charge. Tiger Woods, for example, charges $3 million for playing in tournaments overseas!

Gulf states, flooding the city of New Orleans, killing more than a thousand people and uprooting many more.

Like many people, Michelle reacted to the hurricane disaster with concern and generosity. She presented the $500,000 to none other than former president Bill Clinton a few weeks later. After giving him the check, Wie even got to play a round of golf with Clinton.

What did Michelle think of her experience? "It was really awesome," Wie said later. "It was really cool to see a former president."

LIFE AS A PRO

So what changed for Michelle after she turned pro? Well for one thing, not too many amateurs travel with stylists, image consultants, and sports psychologists. But then again, as Eric Adelson of *ESPN: The Magazine,* points out, Michelle already had all of these things. "Wie already acts like a pro, spending two-and-a-half hours on most weekdays at one of three Honolulu courses," he wrote. "On weekends, she's at the course for six hours per day. On Tuesdays, she gets a massage (plus manicure/pedicure). She has a strength trainer who sends her workouts, a sports psychologist with whom she speaks by phone every week, and a nutritionist who tells her what to eat and what to avoid."

So to some extent, life hasn't changed all that much. Except now she's playing for much bigger stakes.

But how can she be a professional golfer if she's not a member of the LPGA? According to LPGA rules, Michelle can't join the LPGA Tour until she turns eighteen. There have been a few notable exceptions to this, including Aree Song and, more re-

This Is the Kind of Homework I'd Do Any Day

One of the things Michelle has been working on since she turned pro, aside from golf, is her image. She even has an image consultant, David Lipman, who also works with singer Justin Timberlake and actress Angelina Jolie. As Lipman told *Fortune* magazine, "We want to define her physical persona, both on and off the golf course." Not preppy and certainly not stodgy, her style tends more toward youthful, slightly edgy. She's even working with Nike to design golfwear the way she'd like it to be.

For homework, her consultants have her cull magazines like *Us Weekly*, looking for photos of celebrities whom she likes, searching for "Michelle's Style." Her style role model of the moment is Kate Hudson, although Michelle is actually not afraid to create her own style altogether. She shows it on the course already, with her chandelier earrings and hip, flattering outfits.

cently, Morgan Pressel joining the Tour at age seventeen (see chapter 12 for more on Morgan Pressel). But for now, Michelle has no plans to petition to join the LPGA early. She can still play a pretty full schedule of LPGA events, though, because nonmembers are allowed to play in up to eight LPGA events a year. There are several ways this can happen.

Some tournaments give players the opportunity to qualify for their events through "Monday qualifiers"—rounds of golf before the actual tournament begins, where the top finisher wins a spot in the field. Another way is by finishing high in other tournaments. At the USGA-sponsored U.S. Women's Open, for example, the top twenty finishers win an automatic spot in the next year's tournament. And the final way to play in LPGA events without being a member is through sponsor exemptions. LPGA members are officially "exempt" and able to play in LPGA events. But sponsors of tournaments reserve the right to invite a few extra non-Tour members to join a tournament's roster.

Until she turns eighteen, Michelle will continue to accept sponsor exemptions to both LPGA and PGA Tour events and pick up appearance fees at overseas events as well. With that limited schedule, she'll be able to continue her high school studies until she graduates in 2007 and make plenty of money at the same time.

THE GOLF WORLD REACTS

Michelle's family had thought about the decision of when to turn pro for months, even years. With all the success she'd experienced, it was natural for them to think that holding her to an amateur career was just holding her back, period. Her life goal was to play on both the LPGA and the PGA Tours, so why not start now?

It was pretty clear from her performances in 2004 and 2005 that she belonged at that level of competition; she would have earned more than $1 million from those two years alone. In 2005, she had played in just eight events but had four top-five finishes and a second-place finish in a major—an excellent record for a full-time professional, let alone a part-time amateur.

In a press conference, Michelle was asked to explain how

she made her decision to turn pro. She responded, "It all came down to the last couple of months. I felt really ready and very comfortable playing out there. . . . Of course, I mean it took a lot of planning. It took a lot of discussion, talking about, you know, what are the cons and what are the pros of turning pro, and all of a sudden I said, I think I'm ready for it, I really want to do it, and I think I made a pretty good decision."

Michelle's former coach Casey Nakama put it succinctly: "I think it was the right time for her to turn pro. I don't think there was anything else for her to prove as an amateur. Her draw at a tournament, the media attention that she gets, a lot of people want to see her play."

Gary Gilchrist, who worked with Michelle at the David Leadbetter Academy until 2004, agrees. "I think she might as well turn pro now because she doesn't play junior golf," he says.

But not everyone thought turning pro was a good decision. While some of her golfing heroes, such as Ernie Els, encouraged Michelle, others, such as Annika Sorenstam, thought she'd be better off focusing on her junior career first.

As Annika told Dave Allen of *GOLF Magazine,* "If it were my kid, I'd recommend she play more junior events to learn how to win. I do think it's very important to play with better players and learn from that, but I don't think you necessarily have to be in competition to do that. She has no junior record. And you don't get that chance back. It's definitely important to learn how to win, and you can't come back in ten years and say, 'Hey, I missed my whole junior career.' She'll have plenty of time to do the other stuff as well."

Michelle's coach Gary Gilchrist offered his thoughts on this question. "The hard part for her is she became such a prodigy or such a celebrity so early," he says. "The junior events were kind of difficult. The hard part for her, when she got there, was that the other girls were wanting to beat her so badly. I think at times, it would've been a little easier for her if she had learned how to dominate. There is an advantage to those other girls that have learned to win. At any level—it is a help. Is it going to hurt Michelle Wie? Only time will tell. But she's going to have to get to a point in her life where she's playing golf to win, not playing golf because it's just fun for her. Because once you take the money, you're not a sweet little girl anymore. You're another professional golfer that is expected to win. Especially if you get paid a whole bunch of money. Then you're expected to not just win but to dominate."

But the decision to turn pro wasn't made by Michelle alone. She and her family, as they generally do, made the decision together. As her father, BJ, explained to the press, "All three of us, Bo and me and Michelle, made a decision about turning pro. We all considered the different scenarios, the possibilities, what if that happens. We were more concerned about her future than anyone else."

TEN-MILLION-DOLLAR BABY

Going pro turned Michelle into not just the highest-paid female *golfer* in the world but also the third-highest-paid female *athlete* in the world, behind tennis stars Maria Sharapova and Serena Williams.

In their February 2006 issue, *Golf Digest* listed Michelle as fifteenth on the annual world earnings ranking for 2005 although she didn't earn a dime on the course—and that includes *all* professional golfers, male and female.

Going Pro

According to *Fortune* magazine, Michelle could make $10 million in just *one year* as a pro, combining her sponsorship deals, overseas appearance fees, and prize money.

For many golfers, this kind of money can spell trouble: More cash equals more pressure. Now it's not just herself she must please; she must also consider sponsors, tournament organizers, the LPGA, the PGA Tour, and all of her fans. For that kind of money, people say, she'd better be good!

But Michelle insists that the money doesn't pressure her, it motivates her. Whereas once she could look forward to earning five dollars for each birdie, now she can expect much, much more. "I don't feel any pressure at all," she said at a press conference. "I see it as incentive. I'm just loving every moment of this life, you know. It's great."

SO WHAT IS a sixteen-year-old supposed to do with all that money? After all, the average sixteen-year-old doesn't have much to shop for beyond school clothes and movie tickets. They don't usually have to worry about portfolios and stock dividends, long-term investments, or capital gains.

Michelle's parents decided early on that Michelle shouldn't have to, either. So they've put Michelle's earnings into a trust that she won't be able to touch until she's older. (In fact, they can't touch the money, either.)

So Michelle will have to wait a little longer before she can buy that silver Audi TT she's been eyeing. Until then, she'll have to settle for her usual monthly allowance and the cash she wins off her dad's friends—five dollars a hole for eighteen holes.

10

Michelle's Professional Debut: The Samsung World Championship

The rules are the rules. Three inches or 100 yards, it's the same thing. I respect that.

All eyes were on Michelle at her first professional tournament, and she chose it carefully—the 2005 Samsung World Championship. The Samsung World Championship, played at Bighorn Golf Club in Palm Desert, California, is a little different from most LPGA events. For one thing, it doesn't include the entire LPGA. The Samsung World Championship is a special "boutique" tournament that invites only twenty players, the best of the LPGA. For another, there's no cut—everyone who makes it into the tournament earns money.

So Michelle would be joined on the field by just nineteen other LPGA players, the rest of whom were invited based on their current standing on the LPGA money list or their past tournament wins.

The year before, Michelle had tied for thirteenth place at the Samsung; but as an amateur, she had to pass up the check for $15,500 that she would have been entitled to as a pro. This time, she'd be able to keep every penny of her earnings.

As she was a professional now, Michelle and her family felt that it was important to hire a professional caddie, rather than have her father on the bag. So they hired Greg Johnston, who had formerly been LPGA pro Juli Inkster's caddie.

Michelle's first round of the tournament on Thursday, October 13, was fairly uneventful. She played a solid round without mistakes and ended up with a score of 70.

The following day, Friday, Michelle birdied her way to a fantastic 65, which left her tied for second with Annika Sorenstam and Paula Creamer, just two strokes behind the lead.

Saturday, day 3 of the tournament, started off ugly. In just three holes, because of a bogey, then a double bogey, Michelle was already three strokes over par. A birdie on hole number 6, then three more on the back nine, brought her back to a score of 71, much to her relief.

By the end of the final round on Sunday, Michelle was exhausted. But also elated—her final round of 74 was good enough for a fourth-place finish, a perfectly respectable performance for a brand-new professional and one that came with a $53,126 award. She was ready to clean up, change clothes, and head out to the Sweet 16 birthday party that her uncle was hosting later that night.

But she was in for a nasty surprise.

A RUDE AWAKENING

The Wies knew something was wrong when, just minutes after Michelle signed her final-round scorecard, they were approached by rules officials. The officials, Jim Haley and Robert O. Smith, had questions about a drop Michelle had taken during the third round the day before.

On hole number 7, a par 5, Michelle had tried to reach the green in just two strokes. It was an aggressive play, but if a player is a long hitter, and accurate as well, reaching the green in two shots is often the best way to make birdies. Unfortunately, Michelle's approach shot missed the green and ended up under a bush. Under the rules of golf, players are allowed to declare a ball "unplayable" and drop the ball in a better spot (as long as the spot they choose is no closer to the hole), with a one-stroke penalty.

Michelle had pulled her ball out from under the Gold Lantana bush and dropped it within two club-lengths in a patch of grass next to the bush, feeling confident that the ball was no closer to the hole than it had been when it was still under the bush. Her first drop seemed to roll closer, so she dropped it again.

She had then chipped her ball onto the green and made her 15-foot putt, resulting in a par save that had her breathing a sigh of relief. No player likes to take an unplayable lie, because the penalty—an extra stroke on your card—can make your score balloon.

At the time all seemed fine. Her caddie thought the drop was done correctly, as did her playing partner that day, Grace Park. Although Michelle had the right to request a rules official to come give her drop his blessing, she had decided that wasn't necessary; for one thing, she and Grace were falling behind the rest of the players and needed to speed up their round, and calling for a rules official would use up valuable minutes. For another, Michelle has taken many drops in her golf career and she felt confident that she could tell a proper drop from an improper one.

But there was someone in the gallery who felt uneasy about her drop. As Michelle later discovered, a reporter who was following Michelle around the course, Michael Bamberger of *Sports Illustrated,* thought something wasn't right.

Bamberger, standing 6 feet behind Michelle as she pulled the ball from the bush, had doubts. To his eyes, the ball appeared closer to the hole. Uncertain of what to do, he waited until the group had finished up; then he stayed behind and paced off the distance to the flag from the bush, then from her drop. By his measurement, her drop came up short—it was one pace closer to the hole.

Here's where things start to get tricky.

Golf is a funny sport. With most sports, the rules are enforced by referees or umpires, officials who watch every piece of the action and stop play any time they observe a breach of the rules. But with golf, players act as their own referees. If they have questions, they can call a rules official, who can help clarify an issue. But there's no one standing next to each group blowing a whistle at every foul.

Instead, players police themselves and one another, and sometimes, strangely enough, the gallery, fans, and random observers help out, and can change the outcome of the tournament by doing so.

In this case, Bamberger felt strongly enough that Michelle had broken the rules that he reported the violation to rules officials—but by the time he did so, not only had Michelle finished her round and signed her scorecard, but she had finished the following day's round, too.

On Sunday, after the tournament was over and everyone's results were in, Bamberger contacted the rules officials, Haley and Smith, and asked them to review Saturday's drop.

Concerned, the officials reviewed videotape from the previous day but couldn't tell for sure if the drop had been proper or not. So a few minutes after Michelle turned in her final-round scorecard, the officials asked her to accompany them back to the seventh green, where the alleged violation took place. Michelle and her caddie made a guess as to where the ball had been in the bush and where she had made the drop.

First, the officials paced off the drop, but they were still unable to tell for sure whether the drop was closer or farther from the hole. So they pulled out measuring string and compared the two distances.

Unfortunately for Michelle, the answer was now clear: She had dropped the ball closer to the hole—12 to 15 inches closer, according to the officials.

BREAKING THE RULES

Now Michelle was in violation of several rules. First was Rule 28, which states: "If the player deems his ball to be unplayable, he must, under penalty of one stroke: a. Play a ball as nearly as possible at the spot from which the original ball was last played; or b. Drop a ball behind the point where the ball lay, keeping that point directly between the hole and the spot on which the ball is dropped, with no limit to how far behind that point the ball may be dropped; or c. Drop a ball within two club-lengths of the spot where the ball lay, but not nearer the hole."

Michelle had opted for c, dropping the ball within two club-lengths of the spot where the ball lay, but not nearer the hole. Since it was determined that the ball was in fact closer, Rule 28 had clearly been broken, which calls for a two-stroke penalty.

But more important, she had broken Rule 6-6, which states: "The competitor is responsible for the correctness of the score recorded for each hole on his scorecard. If he returns a score for any hole lower than actually taken, he is disqualified."

Because she should have received a score of 7 on the hole, rather than the 5 that she had reported, and because she had officially signed her scorecard with the incorrect score, she was disqualified.

Ouch! What a blow—her first professional tournament, and she was painfully, embarrassingly, disqualified. Instead of a check for more than $53,000, she received nothing.

This was big news in the golf world. Michelle was immediately ushered into a press conference to explain what had happened. Reporters peppered her with questions: "Do you agree with this decision?" "How far ahead was the ball?" "When did you find out there might be a problem? When were you first told?" "Can you describe your emotions right now?"

Crushed, Michelle talked through the decision. "Me and Greg [Johnston, her caddie] were talking when we were up at the shot," she explained. "He told me to watch out, that you're not closer. I made sure that I was farther. Well, I thought I was farther behind. But it looked fine to me. And it was far away. You know, it looked fine to me. I didn't have any question in my mind that I was ahead of the line. . . . It was all guesswork where the ball was, where the ball was yesterday, where the ball was originally in the bushes. . . . I'm pretty sad but, you know, I think I'm going to get over it. I learned a lot from it. It's obviously not the way I wanted to begin but, you know, it's all right."

Now Michelle was front-page news again, but for all the wrong reasons.

TO TELL OR NOT TO TELL

Interestingly, Michelle wasn't the only person under fire. Many people took issue with the man who blew the whistle, the *Sports Illustrated* reporter who originally thought Michelle had made a bad drop, and ultimately blamed him for getting her disqualified.

It wasn't just Michelle's fans who were mad at Bamberger. Leonard Shapiro, a sports columnist for *The Washington Post,* wrote an article called "Rulings Are for Officials, Not Reporters," saying: "Back in Journalism 101, among the first principles ever driven into our young and fertile minds was the concept that reporters should never become part of the story. We're there to report and write about what we witnessed, but not inject ourselves into the action or contribute to altering the basic facts of what we've just seen or heard.

"But affecting the outcome of a golf tournament because you believe a rules violation has taken place goes way above and beyond the role of the sports press. . . . As a journalist, he had no right, no matter what sort of moral high ground he has been taking in all the interviews I've seen him give since the DQ, to insinuate himself into the story. He was out of line. Period and end of story."

Sports Illustrated defended Bamberger's actions. Senior

writer Alan Shipnuck wrote *SI*'s response to the incident, saying: "Bamberger had a sleepless night on Saturday knowing that if he reported Wie, and if it was determined that she had broken a rule, she would be disqualified. It would be unprecedented for a reporter to affect the outcome of a tournament in such a manner, but Bamberger felt compelled to pursue the matter. 'Adherence to the rules is the underlying value of the game,' Bamberger says. 'To stand in silence when you see an infraction is an infraction itself.'"

Shipnuck went on to point out: "Every week the PGA Tour receives multiple phone calls from TV viewers who think they have spotted infractions. To some, spectators who report violations are busybodies. In fact, third parties—even reporters—who point out rules infractions are protecting the field and preserving the integrity of the competition."

But even Bamberger seemed uncertain about his actions. He was fully aware that, as a journalist who had changed the outcome of the event he was reporting on, he was on shaky ground.

In an interview with fellow *SI* writers, he said, "In hindsight, if I could do anything over again, I would try to intercept her between the eighteenth green and her signing the scorecard. I wish I would have done that." If he had, Michelle would have been assessed a simple two-stroke penalty rather than disqualification.

The following week, *Sports Illustrated* editors mentioned that the magazine had received more than twelve hundred letters about the incident. All but a handful, the magazine claimed, were critical of Bamberger and *SI*.

Michelle might be comforted to know that she was supported by her old instructor Casey Nakama, who said, "As players, we are responsible for the rules. The bottom line is she is responsible for that, between her and her caddie, so it should've never happened. But—the process of what had happened, Michael Bamberger, if he knew golf as much as they said he did, he wrote a book and caddied for a year, he knew that he should've made that call before the end of that day. He should've said something at the end of the round before she signed that card. That was just poor judgment on his part. He should've made that call before Saturday or just not said anything at all. The timing of the whole thing was wrong."

Regardless of the outcome and regardless of how fair or unfair it may have been, Michelle learned a valuable lesson. She ended her press conference saying, "Obviously, I was really disappointed with my first event. But, you know, at least I got it out of the way. . . . I learned my lesson, I'm going to call a rule official every single time."

SMALL CONSOLATION

A few days after her disappointment at the Samsung World Championship, Michelle received a pick-me-up in the form of a text message from Annika Sorenstam. Michelle's father, BJ, told *USA Today*, "Annika was not happy to hear of Michelle's disqualification. She encouraged her to keep her chin up and not to get frustrated or disappointed. They were comforting words. Michelle was pretty quiet, but after getting the message from Annika, she was excited." Annika's runaway eight-shot victory at the Samsung—her sixty-fourth career victory—had been somewhat overshadowed by Michelle's disqualification, but she didn't let that stop her from expressing sympathy for what she felt was a raw deal.

Michelle's Professional Debut

CERTAINLY MICHELLE ISN'T the first player in golf's history to be disqualified. It happens more often than you might think. In fact, golf lore is loaded with stories of disqualifications not unlike what happened to Michelle.

Just ask PGA Tour professional Craig Stadler. In 1987, finding himself having to hit a ball out from under a tree, he decided to hit the shot from his knees. But the ground was muddy and he didn't want to dirty his pants, so he spread out a towel to kneel on.

No big deal, right? Wrong. According to Rule 13-3, kneeling on a towel falls under the category of "building a stance"— and carries a two-stroke penalty. An alert viewer watching a TV replay the following day realized this, phoned in a complaint to NBC, and next thing you know, Craig Stadler was disqualified. Not for building a stance, but for signing an incorrect scorecard, just like Michelle. As Robert O. Smith, the rules official who disqualified Michelle, said, "Once that scorecard is signed, it's history."

And of course, not every player who gets disqualified has someone else blowing the whistle on them. Sometimes players blow the whistle on themselves! At the 2005 Office Depot Championship, LPGA Rookie of the Year Paula Creamer realized she had placed a new club in her bag during an overnight rain delay—another no-no that breaks Rule 4-4, which states: "The player must start a stipulated round with not more than 14 clubs. He is limited to the clubs thus selected for that round." She didn't wait for anyone to point this out to officials—she paid the piper and disqualified herself, forfeiting the $11,859 check she would have won for her twenty-third-place finish.

Who Wrote the Rules?

According to the United States Golf Association, the USGA, in conjunction with its European counterpart, the Royal and Ancient in Scotland, "writes, interprets, and maintains the Rules of Golf to guard the tradition and integrity of the game. The two organizations are joint authors and owners of the Rules of Golf and Decisions on the Rules of Golf."

SCORECARD WOES

There is one scenario whereby you could sign an incorrect scorecard and not be disqualified—that's if you gave yourself a higher score than what you actually made. If that's the case, you're not disqualified, but the higher score stands. And in professional golf tournaments, you don't mark your own card; your playing partner does. So if your playing partner gives you the wrong (lower) score and you sign the card, you're disqualified. And if they write down the wrong (higher) score and you sign the card, your score is whatever you signed for.

The most famous example of this was at the 1968 Masters. In that horrible episode, Roberto DeVicenzo made a birdie—a 3—on the seventeenth hole during the final round. But his playing partner marked down a 4. After the round, DeVicenzo signed his card without noticing the error. His 67 turned into a 68. He should have tied for the lead and gone into a play-off. Instead, that one extra stroke cost him the chance for the title.

11

There's Always Room for Improvement

I'm ready to take on any new challenges.

Even with her prodigious talent, Michelle has to work very hard to stay on top of her game. She can't just sit back and relax, no matter how good she is. She's always looking to improve. When Michelle first started working with Casey Nakama at age nine, she was tall and strong and could bomb the ball 300 yards. But her drives went everywhere—into the water, into the woods, out-of-bounds. It took time and effort to get her drives under control.

Three years later, when she began working with Gary Gilchrist at the David Leadbetter Golf Academy, she still had quite a bit of work to do. She had already been the youngest to qualify for an LPGA event and played with PGA Tour professionals, but it wasn't enough—she had set a lofty goal, to play on the PGA Tour (as well as the LPGA), and knew she still had a long way to go.

Even now, although she's a professional golfer, although

she's played in twenty-seven LPGA events to date and four PGA Tour events, although she earns millions of dollars in endorsements, she has to continue to work on her game—actually, she has to work on it *because* of those things.

So what's her secret? How does she just keep getting better and better? And when will she ever be good enough?

It has to do with motivation. When she first began taking lessons at age nine, Casey Nakama didn't notice anything particularly special about her. He saw in front of him a strong girl, tall for her age, but not necessarily a superstar.

But she was a quick learner, and before long she had shown that she loved to compete. Once she started to compete, and win, she was willing to put in whatever amount of time and effort it would take to make it to the next level.

Nakama knew he was working with a different breed when he gave her his first sand lesson. If you're a golfer, you know that bunker shots can be the most difficult—you can hack away, again and again, and never get the ball out of the sand.

With Michelle, Nakama demonstrated what she should do and after her third try she was making the correct movement. "That's when I really remember shaking my head, when I came in after that lesson. I thought that was really unusual for a player to be able to do that," Nakama recalls. "I think she was only ten years old."

While most of his clients stand somewhere in the vicinity of 4'6" (his youngest students are just seven years old), Michelle, at age nine, was already 5'7". Because of her height Nakama had her keep her arms away from her body and kept her swing arc big, with a large shoulder turn.

Golf turned out to be the perfect sport for Michelle. She had tried other sports—baseball, soccer, basketball—and even excelled, but there was too much running involved. Michelle is not a fan of running.

In golf, players don't really have to break a sweat. Strength is certainly a plus, but precision and skill trump all. So with plenty of practice, Michelle could hone her game to the point of becoming an exceptional player for her age. And practice, unlike running, was something she enjoyed.

She took a private lesson with Nakama once a week and in between worked on her game by herself. He gave her suggestions for what to do during her practice sessions but found that he really didn't need to; she would spend hours on the range without being told.

Under Nakama's tutelage, Michelle's game bloomed. She went from an average junior player to a girl among men in just two years. By age ten she had shot a 64. By age twelve she had qualified for an LPGA event, the Takefuji Classic, becoming the youngest female ever to do so, and won the Jennie K. Wilson Invitational, beating Hawaii's best female amateurs—women three times her age.

At that point Michelle could have sat back and relaxed, and enjoyed what she had already accomplished at such a young age. But that's not Michelle's style. Her aim is to keep improving. She had a big dream in mind—to play on both the LPGA and the PGA tours—and she knew it would take constant work to get there.

Then when her new coach came calling—Gary Gilchrist of the David Leadbetter Golf Academy in Florida—Michelle's game moved to the next level. As Gilchrist says, "The Wies were always in a learning frame of mind, what can we learn, what can we improve."

Several times a year Michelle and her family made the trek

out to Florida to train with Gilchrist. At the David Leadbetter Golf Academy, Michelle worked on increasing her drive distance, increasing her fitness, and the biggest thing (according to Gilchrist), improving her putting. In Hawaii, most courses use just one type of grass on their greens—Bermuda bent grass. But in the tournaments Michelle would play on the mainland, she would encounter many other types of greens, and she needed to learn to control her speed accordingly.

"When kids are young they get so aggressive they hit the ball through the break," says Gilchrist. "That's what she did again and again and again, which cost her. Or she'll get tentative and not hit it hard enough. Every tournament we'd look and see and evaluate what could happen. But basically what used to hold her back was momentum on the greens. With fast greens you're going to have to hit the ball with more break and less green. And that for a teenager is quite tough to do."

Good putting comes only through hours and hours of practice. Of course, with anything that requires that much repetition, there's a danger it can get boring. So Gilchrist tried to make it as interesting as possible. "We used to go through many different drills, like putting around a hole, you'd have to use your imagination and putt from different distances," he recalls.

But what Gilchrist worked on most was confidence. He wanted her to focus less on winning and more on improving, bit by bit. "I've always said to them, you need to spend the next three to four years learning and improving. Everything is good, as long as you don't overdo it. The thing I was trying to do with her was make her confident within herself, not in me."

Being Fit to the Core

If you're into fitness, you've probably heard of "core training." In golf, core training is the next big thing, superseding just about any other element of fitness training. What is the core? Most people think of just the abdominals when they think of the core, but it's more than that. The core encompasses many muscle groups on the front, side, and backside of the body. It consists of the muscles that make up your abdominals, lower back, obliques, and hips.

Why is the core so important to golf? The core is where the golf swing's power comes from. A strong core equals a strong swing, with more distance and accuracy.

Golfers these days work the core using a variety of exercises, and a lot of them involve a "stability ball." Have you seen one of those in your gym—those big balls that look like a giant Hippity-Hop?

Because a stability ball is unstable—rolling around as you lie on it—it forces you to use more muscles and balance to stay on.

VIDEO LESSONS?

Because Michelle lived in Hawaii but trained with a coach who lived in Florida, she couldn't get the daily one-on-one attention that his other students received. No worries, though. That's what technology is for—in this case, a video camera. To maximize her practice time with specific goals or to make needed adjustments, her parents would videotape her swing, she would e-mail Gilchrist the video clips, and he and Leadbetter would then review and comment.

Videotape analysis of the golf swing has been around for a while, but long-distance lessons are something relatively new.

Says Gilchrist, "Because BJ is a professor, they come from a background that's very analytical; it's like there's a magic formula you can have to be a champion. So if she started hitting the ball a little to the left, a little to the right, they'd ask for help. They spent so much time on the range hitting balls, they wanted to make sure it was quality practice, real specific."

Michelle needn't have worried quite so much, according to Gilchrist: "I don't think you need a perfect swing to win. At the end of the day it all boils down to heart. You have to have the heart of a champion. What makes the greatest players comes from within, not from without."

Casey Nakama would agree. In fact, he's worried that her swing at this point may be suffering from too much tinkering; while Michelle needs to continue to work on her game, he says, she'll need to be careful to filter out what helps her game and what ultimately hurts it: "I think they've [Leadbetter and Gilchrist] mechanized her swing a little bit more. I always want players to have feel in their movement, I want their swing to be a little bit more flowing. They seem to be real mechanical and position oriented. So it's a lot more stiffer in how she's swing-ing it. . . . It's helped her just with information, but when you eventually have to put things together in this game, when you have a player that's more mechanical than a feel player, the feel player will always play better."

At the end of 2004, Gary Gilchrist left the David Leadbetter Golf Academy to make a name for himself elsewhere, at the International Junior Golf Academy in Hilton Head Island, South Carolina. But Michelle has continued to train at the DLGA, now under Leadbetter himself.

It was a decision that involved all parties: BJ, Bo, Michelle, Gilchrist, and Leadbetter. "I felt at that time, and BJ felt at that time, that David would be the right person to take her from one level to the next," explains Gilchrist. "David brings not just his instruction but also the players that he teaches. She has practice rounds with Ernie Els and [2005 PGA Rookie of the Year] Sean O'Hair. They are both David's students. What a great opportunity that is."

Michelle now has an entire entourage of specialists who help her train. Leadbetter helps her with her swing; Paul Gagne helps her with fitness; Jim Loehr helps her with sports psychology.

All that information can help a lot—or it can hurt a lot. Gilchrist worries sometimes that for now, at least, it's too much to take in. "There's too many people now giving her so much information," he says. "When I was with her, I only spoke when I thought it was necessary. But now she's got some of the best—the best mental coach, the best physical coach, and the best technical teacher—all of them giving information, it just becomes overwhelming. At the end of the day, she needs to spend time on her own, and think on her own. And that's going to take time. She's got to basically grow into a young woman and learn when to take information and when not to take information."

David Leadbetter, who writes regularly for *Golf Digest,* explained that his purpose in working with Michelle wasn't to overtinker but to help her understand her own swing. "When a coach gets the chance to work with an incredible raw talent like Michelle, it's really a case of guiding and channeling that talent—a tweak here, a tweak there, and let her get on with it," he wrote.

What Exactly Is a Sports Psychologist?

It sounds kind of funny, doesn't it—sports psychologist? But you'd be surprised how many athletes use them. Many athletes find that problems in their game come from not a physical breakdown but a mental one. Negative thoughts, too much stress, getting down on yourself for a poor performance, all of these can cause long-lasting, potentially career-ending problems. Sports psychologists promise an extra edge—mental toughness—that appeals to high-level athletes.

A sports psychologist works with elite athletes to help keep them in a relaxed state of mind. They might do this by telling golfers to forget about score and just have fun on the course or to set small goals for themselves—"with this shot, think only about placing the ball next to that tree."

Most sports psychologists who work with golfers agree that a major issue is confidence: If a golfer doesn't believe the ball is going to go in the hole, then it won't. Simply reminding themselves that it was a bad shot, rather than declaring themselves to be bad players, can make a big difference.

Michelle has been working with psychologist Jim Loehr since the end of 2004. Dr. Loehr, founder of a company called LGE Performance Systems, is a hot commodity these days—he works with business executives, law enforcement teams, and professional athletes (including golfers Mark O'Meara and Nick Faldo and tennis stars Monica Seles and Jim Courier). He's even appeared on *The Oprah Winfrey Show*.

Like Michelle's lessons with Leadbetter, her sessions with Loehr take place mainly by e-mail and phone. Loehr told *For-*

tune magazine that he has told her to lighten up a little, play a little bit less golf to give herself a break, and enjoy the time on the course more. He even tells her to repeat to herself things like, "I'm the best putter in the history of golf."

"You can tell she enjoys what she's doing," Loehr told *Golf Digest*. "The whole deal for her is to have fun if no one will allow her to be anything other than extraordinary."

Loehr also pointed out that Michelle has set a monumental task for herself: that of not just being a world-class golfer but also breaking down barriers. "What impressed me as far as her future is concerned is how self-directed she is. In our first meeting, she articulated that she considers herself to be on a mission, one that will communicate to women that there really are no boundaries."

Leadbetter and Gilchrist both found that Michelle was almost *too* flexible—at the end of her fluid backswing, her club ended up farther than parallel to the ground. Explains Leadbetter in an article: "This caused her arms to swing down late and too far from the inside, resulting in both hooks and blocks as her hands tried to catch up."

So to improve her consistency, Leadbetter had Michelle adjust her swing so that it was a bit shorter. That, he wrote, "had a ripple effect through to the finish. Her arms and body got more in sync. . . . Now her hands need not be so active."

Fitness has been another thing Leadbetter has stressed—for more length on the course and also to prevent injury. He's the one who brought in fitness guru Paul Gagne to help train Michelle. "Michelle tended to shy away from it [strength training]," said Leadbetter. "But once we pointed out the benefits, it's a full program she has to work on. When you've got the talent she has, it's a matter of getting your ducks in a row. She's game for it. She's starting to enjoy it."

"The fitness has been pretty tough," Michelle admitted at a press conference. "I had Paul come over [to Hawaii] for a week. The workout was very intense. I couldn't wash my hair in the

What's Swing Speed?

Swing speed, or clubhead speed, as it's also referred to, is the speed at which your club is traveling when it hits the ball. Don't make the mistake many golfers do and confuse it with the speed with which you whip your arms around.

Why worry about swing speed? It is the main component in getting your ball to travel farther—greater swing speed equals greater distance. It's also one of the reasons men are generally able to hit golf balls farther than women—the average man can generate far more clubhead speed than can the average woman.

According to Callaway, a leading equipment manufacturer, the average recreational female golfer has a swing speed between 60 and 70 miles per hour, which is about 20 to 30 mph slower than the average recreational male.

What about professionals? Tiger Woods, John Daly, and Hank Kuehne lead the way on the PGA Tour, averaging about 130 mph. But the average PGA Tour pro swing speed is closer to about 115 mph. Michelle, meanwhile, averages about 105 mph, about the same as Annika Sorenstam.

shower—it was way too painful. I couldn't lift my arms. My New Year's resolution is to cut down sugar and not be as lazy. That means going to the gym a lot more. My goal is to get fit, get stronger, and prevent injury. Paul has been very helpful in that sense."

With Gagne's guidance, Michelle has already gained eight pounds of muscle, which will be critical in helping her increase her swing speed. Like the disgusting Korean concoction made with goat and snake juice that her mother used to make her drink, exercise has become the necessary evil to take Michelle to the next level. And that's what Michelle is always looking to do—move to the next level.

But more than anything else, Michelle's coaches have encouraged her to do the one thing that will most improve her game: play against men. It's one of the reasons that she's so well-known—a female regularly playing against men is something that hasn't been done since Babe Didrikson Zaharias did it more than sixty years ago. It's thinking outside the box, and the sports world is at once both fascinated and uncomfortable with the idea.

Michelle's dream is to be one of the best in the world, and to achieve that dream, Gilchrist points out, she must play against the best in the world, including men. "There's no way she can beat the men by simply playing on the LPGA. If you want to be known as one of the best golfers in the world, you're going to have to play the men."

While it remains to be seen whether she will ever beat the men or even make a cut, one thing is clear: Playing against men improves her game.

"Playing PGA Tour events makes her better," Leadbetter has said. "I think she gets psyched watching the guys and seeing their ability. It raises her level. It helps her up the ladder of improvement."

Michelle agrees. As she said in a press conference before the 2006 Sony Open, "Playing with the guys has made me a better player. With that experience and knowledge, I think it will help me win women's events. That's my goal—to win the women's events."

At the PGA Tour's Bank of America Colonial in 2003, Annika Sorenstam made headlines by accepting an invitation to play with the guys. She shot 71-74 to miss the cut but to this day gives credit to that single tournament for improving her game.

Before the Colonial, she won 22 percent of the LPGA events she entered. In the two and a half years following, her win rate increased to 46 percent.

"If you look at Colonial, I only played for two days, but the experience I got there is for a lifetime," Annika told *Golf Today*. "That's really what I think is helping me sit here today, all of the wins I've had since. I prepared for three and a half months for that, which was a lot of weight training, a lot of fine-tuning on my swing, a lot of hard work on my short game. I wouldn't say it paid off that particular week, but it paid off down the road, for sure." Perhaps it was the actual experience during those two days, or perhaps it was the level of intense practice she put into preparing for it; either way, playing against men has made Annika Sorenstam a better player—one of the best in the history of women's golf.

Leadbetter points out that Michelle's ability already exceeds that of most other females. "She doesn't play as many tournaments as other girls her age," he told the Associated Press. "I guarantee there's a lot of girls on the AJGA who play a heck of a lot more tournaments than Michelle does. But when you limit the number of tournaments you play, and you play the best men and women, your chances of winning are less. She can win with a half set of clubs in her bag [on the AJGA]. These girls are good, but this girl is special."

And Leadbetter doesn't limit his comments to amateurs; he has also claimed that Michelle's game exceeds that of most female professionals. "The thing she has over all the other girls is great shot making," Leadbetter has said. "She can draw it, fade it, and around the green she has a tremendous variety of shots. . . . Obviously, that's why Annika enjoys playing with Tiger, because he helps her with the short game." Playing with someone such as Tiger, Leadbetter argues, has brought Annika to a new level. In the same way, playing with PGA Tour players teaches Michelle things she can't learn playing against women.

But while it may be helping Michelle's game, playing on the men's tour is not necessarily helping her relationship with other female players. Many LPGA players see Michelle's desire to play on the PGA Tour to be nothing more than hubris—an overinflated sense that she is so special, she can skip women's golf altogether. Who does she think she is? they ask themselves.

Beth Daniel, for example, an icon on the LPGA Tour, winner of thirty-three tournaments, did not appreciate David Leadbetter's remarks that Michelle's shot making is something "she has over all the other girls."

"That just got my blood pressure up," Beth told *USA Today*. "You couldn't tell me that Mickey Wright couldn't hit it right and left and high and low, and Karrie Webb couldn't do that. All of us who have played on our tour are capable of hitting those golf shots. For him to make a comment like that and people are reading that and thinking, 'Wow, she's the only woman who can do that.' That's the perception that's given up."

Michelle's former coach Casey Nakama was a little more careful in his remarks to the press, realizing they could be taken the wrong way. Early on, he even suggested to the Wies that they not be quite so open about Michelle's desire to play on the PGA Tour. Within your own circle, it's fine, he told the Wies, but declaring openly in public that you want to play on the PGA Tour could backfire. "'Aren't we good enough?' the LPGA players will say. With just a simple comment like that, so innocent, she had already created some animosity when she got out on the LPGA Tour," says Nakama.

These days, Michelle has become a bit more guarded in her comments. While Leadbetter might rave that Michelle has more ability than the rest of her female counterparts, Michelle herself makes it clear that she wants to play on *both* tours, the PGA Tour and the LPGA Tour. It's not a question of either/or.

Asked by Mark Rolfing of the Golf Channel which she would prefer, to win a women's tournament or to make the cut in a men's tournament, she responded, "I would choose both. Winning an LPGA tournament would be awesome because it's something I've always wanted to do. And making the cut on the PGA would be a whole different feeling, to be able to do something no one else has ever done."

As long as Michelle is still in high school, making those cuts will be difficult. Right now, she spends as much as two months between tournaments, making it nearly impossible to compete with those players who grind it out every single weekend. Says former coach Gary Gilchrist, "There's no momentum to her golf yet. There's too many gaps. I don't know many pros, no, I

Is Michelle Really the First Woman to Play Against Men?

No, Babe Didrikson Zaharias did it regularly and even made several cuts on the PGA Tour back in 1945 (see chapter 2). As mentioned earlier, Annika Sorenstam played in the Bank of America Colonial in 2003. Later that same year, teaching pro Suzy Whaley qualified for and played in the PGA Tour's Greater Hartford Open but shot 75-78 to miss the cut.

On other tours, four-time LPGA champion Se Ri Pak has had the most success—in 2003 she placed tenth at the SBS Super Tournament, an event on the Korean Tour. Big hitter Laura Davies of England, with twenty LPGA wins (four of which were majors), tried her hand at the Korean Open on the Asian PGA Tour in 2003 but missed the cut by four strokes. Also in 2003, Sweden's Sophie Gustafson played in the Casio World Open in Japan but failed to make the cut.

And most recently, Ai Miyazato, six-time winner on the Japan LPGA and winner of medalist honors at LPGA Qualifying School, played in the Okinawa Open on Japan's JGTO Tour in 2005 but missed the cut.

Playing against men isn't an idea Michelle invented; however, her goal to ultimately play on the PGA Tour is, for now, unique to her.

don't know if there are *any* pros that can take off from golf a month and then go and play in a tournament and do well. She's the only one I've seen do it."

He has faith, however, that one day she'll be competitive,

not just on the women's tour but on the men's as well. "If they can stick with the same equipment, the same caddie, the same team, the information will be consistent, and she will develop into one of the world's greatest players. . . . I still think she'll be the first woman to win on both tours. I still believe she has the game to win a major on both tours, not just a tournament. If she keeps it simple, and keeps a good team around her, she can manage it."

12

Girl Power

*I'm not really sure if there's going
to be a rivalry or not.
I'm not going to think about it.*

GOLF'S "YOUTH MOVEMENT"

Michelle isn't the only famous girl golfer on the block. She's accompanied by seventeen-year-old U.S. Women's Amateur Champion Morgan Pressel, as well as nineteen-year-old Rookie of the Year Paula Creamer, who won her first tournament on the LPGA in 2005, then graduated from high school the following week. This influx of new blood is something unprecedented; in an average year the LPGA might have one teenager climbing their leaderboards, but three? The abilities of these young girls have seasoned LPGA professionals shaking their heads.

With so many opportunities to learn and compete, today's teenagers arrive at the doors of the LPGA with far more experience than did their predecessors. "They have a lot more resources," LPGA player Rosie Jones told *The Sacramento Bee*. "When we came out, we came just raw out of college. Now, with the AJGA [American Junior Golf Association], that gives them a lot more tournament experience. They're a lot more savvy with competition. Teaching is so much better than when I was twelve, thirteen, fourteen. That's when you're most likely to groove your swing. Technology helps them hit super shots at a young age. It's a lot of fun to watch."

And now, thanks to these young guns, the LPGA is riding the crest of a huge wave of popularity. It's become its own reality TV show, and everyone wants to know who's going to end up on top.

The advantages of the LPGA's surge in popularity are clear: 2005 saw the LPGA reach its highest numbers in years in TV ratings and coverage, and it was also the first year that as many as six players hit the $1 million mark. More fans and more viewers equals more sponsors. More sponsors equals bigger purses. Everyone wins.

But with three young stars so close in age competing together in these events, comparisons are inevitable. And because sports fans love rivalries, extra attention has been paid to the relationships among these girls.

MORGAN PRESSEL

As far as rivalries go, you don't have to look too far; Morgan Pressel has been particularly outspoken regarding her feelings about Michelle Wie. Known for showing a little attitude, Pressel's not afraid to share her personality, either on or off the course. In an interview with *Sports Illustrated* in 2005 she said, "I was shocked that there wasn't more talk of Michelle Wie's final round 82 (at the U.S. Women's Open). I mean, why is that? Or how about when it looked like she was going to make the cut at the John Deere Classic, she played the last four holes in

3-over-par. Are the press and other players just trying to be politically correct? I don't believe in being politically correct. Michelle hasn't played a lot of junior golf, so she hasn't learned how to finish tournaments."

After Michelle turned pro and was offered almost $10 million in endorsements, Pressel seemed surprised: "Now, she's going to make something like $10 million? For what? For winning one tournament?" When asked whether Wie would join the LPGA, Pressel exclaimed, "Never. Okay, maybe not never, but not as long as she wants to do her 'woo-woo' thing against the men."

Why would Pressel feel this way? Because of Michelle's popularity, she received literally dozens of invitations from tournament sponsors every year to play in their events. The more she played, the more popular she became. Pressel may have seen this as leaving fewer exemptions for everyone else.

There's also the attention factor: Because Michelle declared a goal of playing not just on the LPGA Tour but also on the PGA Tour, she receives more attention, it seems, than other female golfers. While Morgan Pressel names Annika Sorenstam as her role model, Michelle names Tiger Woods.

Considering that most of the other golfers have beaten Michelle in competition at some point, all that attention might seem unfair. In 2003, at the U.S. Girl's Junior Championship, Morgan beat Michelle in head-to-head match play, 3 and 2. In 2005, the two competitors played in only two of the same tournaments, the Kraft Nabisco Championship and the U.S. Women's Open. At the Kraft Nabisco, Michelle finished with a total score of 288, to tie for fourteenth. Morgan's final score was 290, just two strokes behind Michelle, to tie for nineteenth. At the U.S. Women's Open, Pressel blew Michelle away, with a tie for second place versus Michelle's tie for twenty-third. Morgan shot a full seven strokes better than Michelle. So Pressel likely believes that she is at least as good as Wie, maybe even better. Why should all the attention, then, go to Michelle? Why is it that when a reporter interviews Morgan, they often ask questions about Michelle Wie?

At the U.S. Women's Open qualifiers in 2003, Morgan and Michelle were in a play-off for one of the few remaining spots. "It was kind of funny," Pressel described to the Associated Press later. "As I walked off the green, there must have been fifty people—cameras, everything—standing around her and her family. I just looked back and laughed. I had two local people following me, and they left to talk to Michelle."

On the one hand, Pressel has taken the traditional path to success in golf: She worked her way up through junior competitions, then amateur events, dominating at each step before finally qualifying for LPGA and USGA events. On the other hand, Michelle began accepting exemptions to professional events at age thirteen, virtually skipping junior and amateur competitions. She had her reasons—she wasn't allowed to play junior tournaments before age thirteen, and traveling from Hawaii to the mainland to play amateur events was cost-prohibitive. But to Morgan, it was just Michelle's way of avoiding the possibility of losing in junior events and therefore losing marketability.

MORGAN PRESSEL'S CONTRIBUTIONS to women's golf have been substantial and deserve a close look. "I love to compete. I love the search for perfection. I'm constantly refining things, trying to be as perfect a player as I can be," she told *Golf Digest*.

Blond-haired, green-eyed honor student Morgan was born in Florida in 1988, and she's lived there her whole life. Her résumé is packed with accomplishments: At twelve, she qualified for the U.S. Women's Open. On the AJGA circuit, she won an astounding eleven tournaments. In 2004, the year she turned sixteen, she won the North and South Women's Amateur Championship, and the next year she won the prestigious U.S. Women's Amateur with a 9 and 8 victory over twenty-one-year-old Maru Martinez of Venezuela, one of the most decisive victories in the history of the tournament.

Morgan played in seven professional women's events as an amateur in 2005 and had two top-five finishes, never placing lower than twenty-fifth; the money she would have earned tops $350,000. Most critical was the 2005 U.S. Women's Open. Playing in it for the third time at just seventeen years old, she had the lead and the title in her hands on the final day but had to settle for a tie for second after South Korean Birdie Kim made a miracle bunker shot to win.

After that moment, having come so close to winning a women's major, Morgan decided to forego college and turn professional. Though she had already committed to a full scholarship at Duke University, she couldn't bring herself to go once she realized how competitive she could be on the LPGA Tour.

So rather than go ahead with her college plans, she called Duke's coach, Dan Brooks, a few days after the Open and let him know that she was going to try for the LPGA's Qualifying School.

Says Brooks, "When I was watching the U.S. Open, it was killing me! I knew she wouldn't be able to stay after having this experience—almost winning the U.S. Open. I had a gut feeling

I was going to hear from her, and after about five days, I did."

Having established a relationship with Pressel during the previous year's recruiting efforts, Brooks knew that she would have been a real asset to the Duke women's golf team. He also knew that she would have been a challenge to coach, but a worthwhile challenge. Losing her came as a real blow. "I would've loved to have had her on my team. She has a lot of spirit, let's say. She's very feisty. In fact, she can be downright unpleasant at times on the golf course. She and I had already had a little bit of coach–player stuff and worked through some things. She's a brilliant kid—790 in the math part of the SAT—she's just got so much energy inside. I loved that energy; I love the fire that comes out. Even though I would've had to make sure she toed the line, I would've loved that project."

Before she could join the LPGA, however, Morgan had a pretty big obstacle to overcome: The LPGA requires that all of its members be at least eighteen years old. At that time she was only seventeen, and she wouldn't turn eighteen until the following May.

LPGA bylaws do allow players, in certain instances, to petition for early membership. Back in 2003 Aree Song had been allowed to join the LPGA six weeks before she turned eighteen, and Morgan petitioned the LPGA in June, hoping she would be allowed to do the same rather than have to wait an entire year.

But Ty Votaw, the LPGA's commissioner, had other ideas. Instead of allowing her to join early, he compromised—he allowed her to go ahead and play in the LPGA's annual Q-School tournament. If she made it through Q-School, he said that he would then allow her to become a full member of the LPGA after her eighteenth birthday in May of 2006.

As far as Votaw was concerned, he was doing her a favor. "If

I had said no, she would have had to wait until 2007," he told the press. "We feel the eighteen-year-old age limitation is a good rule. If we're ever going to make an exception we will do so only in extraordinary circumstances."

But Morgan wasn't happy with the decision. On the one hand, it would mean she could go ahead and attempt to qualify, rather than have to wait a year for the next Q-School tournament. On the other hand, the downside was pretty clear—even if she made it through Q-School, any money that she earned during those first few months of 2006 would not count toward her official earnings. Nor would she receive automatic invitations to the tournaments—she would have to rely on sponsor exemptions.

"I'm disappointed," Pressel told *Golfweek*. "I felt that I deserved to play full-time next year. Apparently [Votaw] didn't think so. I don't see how I could be a bad thing for the Tour. I think I could be a very good thing. . . . The bottom line is that when you have someone younger who can play you ought to let them out there."

"We should be happy; that's what [Votaw] told us," added Morgan's grandfather, Herb Krickstein. "In our minds it was a halfway decision."

Pressel plunged ahead with her plans to attend Q-School and played admirably throughout the grueling ninety-hole tournament finals, placing sixth and earning her card.

Meanwhile, luck was with Morgan. In September of 2005, Votaw stepped aside as LPGA commissioner, and Morgan repetitioned Votaw's replacement, Carolyn Bivens. Bivens, reviewing Morgan's impressive résumé and liking her Q-School results, decided to overturn Votaw's decision and allow Morgan immediate full membership into the LPGA.

"The decision we made earlier this year was the right decision at the time, but after additional evaluation of her performance on the LPGA Tour over the last several months and conversations with Morgan and her family, I am now confident she's ready to compete successfully on the LPGA Tour," Bivens explained in a statement.

Morgan was thrilled. Now she would be fully exempt for all LPGA tournaments in 2006, her money would count as official earnings, and she wouldn't have to wait until her birthday before earning "rookie points." Each year, the LPGA chooses a Rookie of the Year, based on each rookie's performance. Even if Morgan had won three tournaments before her birthday in May, none of it would have gotten her any closer to the coveted award.

"Becoming a full-time member of the LPGA is a dream come true," Pressel told the press. "I can't wait for the season to start, and to be able to fully compete and be a part of the rookie race."

And now that she was a professional, she was free to make endorsement deals of her own. Almost immediately she signed a multiyear contract with Callaway, a golf equipment manufacturer, agreeing to use their clubs, balls, and footwear, and she soon made a deal with fashion designer Ralph Lauren to sport his golfwear on the course.

Athleticism runs in Morgan's family. Her father was a hockey player and her mother played varsity tennis at the University of Michigan, winning the Big 10 tennis championship in 1978. Her uncle, Aaron Krickstein, was a teenaged phenomenon himself, a tennis player who at age sixteen was the youngest singles champion on the ATP Tour. At one point, he was even ranked sixth in the world.

What Kind of School Is Q-School?

No, it's not what it sounds like. There are no classrooms, no teachers (except for the ones you bring with you), no essays, and no final exams. Qualifying School isn't a school at all—it's a golf tournament. A multiround, multiday tournament that determines who will earn the right to play on the LPGA.

The number of open spots varies every year—in 2005, only twenty-four cards were given out. Finish in the top twenty-four and you earn a Tour card—meaning you'll be invited to play in LPGA tournaments. Don't and you go home. Top twenty-four, that sounds pretty good, right? Not when you consider how many hundreds of women are competing for one of those twenty-four spots.

And it's not just for amateurs hoping to join the Tour. Q-School is for pros, too—ones who haven't played well enough to retain their card, and pros who want to improve their status on the Tour.

First come the two sectional qualifiers, held in late summer, in California and Florida. Then, finally, in the fall, come finals, held at the LPGA International in Daytona Beach, Florida.

Here's how it works: Sectionals consist of a seventy-two-hole (four-round) qualifying tournament. After two rounds, the top seventy players proceed on, while everyone below seventieth place gets cut. After the final round, everyone besides the top thirty players get cut. Those lucky thirty players from each sectional get to advance to the final qualifying tournament.

At the finals, those sixty total sectional qualifiers, plus Futures Tour professionals attempting to join the LPGA, plus current LPGA players whose status is in danger, all get thrown together. In 2005, 140 players made up the field in the Q-School finals; 63 had advanced through sectionals, 10 players came from the Futures Tour, and 67 of the players were current LPGA members. Only twenty-four fully exempt cards were given out, along with thirty-five "nonexempt" cards. ("Nonexempt" means they get to play a few LPGA tournaments, but not all of them. Nobody wants to end up with nonexempt status, because it means they'll only be "part-time pros." They don't know until the last minute whether they'll be allowed to play, and they don't know ahead of time how many invitations they'll receive. They often even have to play qualifiers to get into a tournament.) While the sectional qualifiers, like most professional golf tournaments, last four days, the finals last five. It's a grueling ninety holes where anything can happen.

Q-School tuition isn't cheap—it costs $3,500 to apply, and you have to have a handicap of 3 or less. And that doesn't count traveling expenses.

When Morgan Pressel entered Q-School at the end of 2005, she wasn't gunning just to get her card—she wanted to win. Paula Creamer had made headlines the year before, becoming the youngest player ever to win, and she won with flair, beating her closest competitor by five strokes.

But Morgan struggled at the sectionals. During the first three rounds she shot 73-72-72 and was in danger of missing the chance to advance. But on the last day, she put up nine birdies to end with a stunning 63 and a guaranteed spot in the finals.

Morgan picked up golf clubs at eight years old, after her grandfather decided she wasn't quite quick enough for tennis. Her grandfather taught her the game at first, and by age ten she was breaking 80. She now trains with Martin Hall, the director of instruction at Ibis Golf & Country Club in West Palm Beach, a *Golf Magazine* Top 100 Teacher who has also worked with Jack Nicklaus and Tom Watson.

In 2003, when Morgan was only fifteen, she lost her mother, Kathy, to breast cancer. Morgan has a notably rocky relationship with her father, so after her mother's death she chose to move in with her grandparents, Herb and Evelyn Krickstein, who have been her guardians ever since. Her younger brother, Mitchell, and younger sister, Madison, meanwhile, live with their father.

Though she's passed up a full golf scholarship from Duke, Morgan still plans to graduate from high school in 2006. She'll start her rookie year on the LPGA while finishing up her senior year at the Saint Andrew's School in Boca Raton, Florida. Exceedingly bright, she has a 3.9 GPA, Advanced Placement classes and all, and keeps her game in shape by playing on the girls' golf team. She closed out her junior career by winning the McDonald's Betsy Rawls Girls Championship, scoring a hole-in-one on the third hole. She ended her amateur career by leading her golf team to its third straight 1A state title.

"I like to compete. I just love it," Pressel has said. "I have to win no matter what I'm doing."

PAULA CREAMER

And what about Paula Creamer? While Michelle and Morgan may have a somewhat spiky relationship, Michelle and Paula

consider themselves good friends. They met while training together under David Leadbetter and have faced each other in
tournaments as well. In 2004, they played together as team-
mates in the Curtis Cup, an experience that they both enjoyed
a great deal.

Yet Paula, too, gets tired of all the hype surrounding Michelle: "It gets old. You look everywhere, and there she is," she
told the *San Francisco Chronicle* at the 2003 U.S. Women's
Open. "I play against the best juniors in the world, and she's
just another junior. I don't place her on a higher plateau."

When coach Gary Gilchrist first met Michelle back in 2002,
he returned to the David Leadbetter Golf Academy excited
about his find. He explains: "When I heard about this young
girl, Michelle Wie, I had another young girl that I also helped
recruit—Paula Creamer. Paula had no competition, and when
I found Michelle Wie, I told Paula's dad, 'I've found a girl who's
going to help, if I can get her here to train, who's going to help
lift the game of women's golf to another level. I'm going to
have a bunch of girls who are going to want to beat each other,
which is going to help challenge them to improve.'" His words
proved prophetic.

Paula, at age nineteen, is the oldest of the threesome that is
credited with comprising the core of golf's "youth movement." She picked up the game at age ten and got serious
about it at age twelve, giving up competitive dance so she
could spend more time on the links. Like Michelle, Paula has
studied at the David Leadbetter Golf Academy for years—her
family moved from California to Florida when she was fourteen so she could train at the DLGA and graduate from
Pendleton, the school associated with the Leadbetter Academy. Like Michelle, Paula works with an entire entourage of

staff: swing instructors David Whelan and David Conatucci, mental conditioning coach Chris Passarella, and media and communications adviser Steve Shenbaum.

All that coaching from such a young age didn't go to waste. When Michelle Wie played with Paula for the first time, Michelle's family was struck by her toughness. Says Gary Gilchrist, "The first thing BJ said in the car was how strong Paula's mind is. They could tell."

Paula's amateur résumé, like Morgan Pressel's, is extensive. She won nineteen amateur titles, including eleven AJGA tournaments. She played in her first LPGA event in 2004 and at age seventeen came in second (by just one shot) in the LPGA's ShopRite Classic and tied for thirteenth at the U.S. Women's Open (along with guess who? Michelle Wie). When Paula went through the LPGA Tour's Qualifying School in 2004, she took first place, making history as the first amateur to win the event outright.

She played extremely well on the LPGA her rookie year, with nine top-five finishes and two wins: the Sybase Classic and the Evian Masters (considered by many to be the Tour's "fifth major" due to its large purse and high-quality field). This bumped her earnings for the year past the million-dollar mark, making her the youngest and fastest player to earn $1 million in career earnings—it took her only four months, twenty-seven days. She also won two events on the Japan LPGA—the NEC Karuizawa and the Masters GC Ladies—and finished the year second on the money list behind Annika Sorenstam, earning more than $1.5 million. By August, Paula had already clinched Rookie of the Year honors, finishing 664 rookie race points ahead of her closest competitor.

Paula's nickname—the Pink Panther—has as much to do

with her killer instinct as it does her propensity for pastels. Her goal is to become the number-one player in the world, and she's already made a good start.

While Michelle faces ample competition from Paula and Morgan, there are plenty of other players in the mix as well. Although they're no longer teens, Ai Miyazato, Brittany Lang, Virada Nirapathpongporn, Aree and Naree Song, and several other young women have brought attention to themselves with strong play at a young age.

WHAT SPAWNED THIS youth movement? And what will come of it? Ron Sirak of Golf World posed the theory that we have Tiger Woods to thank. "Pressel, for example, started golf as an eight-year-old in 1996, the summer Woods turned pro and signed lucrative endorsement deals," Sirak wrote in the July 8, 2005, issue. "It is not a stretch to say Woods' ability to make the game cool put golf clubs in the hands of better athletes who, a few years earlier, might have opted for a tennis racquet, soccer ball or basketball hoop instead. Pressel, Creamer and Wie are the golfing children of Tiger Woods."

If we can credit Tiger Woods with this influx of new golfing talent, what will this group of young women, in their turn, one day be credited for? How many little girls are watching Morgan Pressel, Paula Creamer, and Michelle Wie reach for the stars and are saying to themselves, "I want to do that"?

13

Playing in the Pros

I always wanted to be known as
doing stuff that no one ever
thought of. I just want to push
myself to the limit.

So what is life like for Michelle now that she's a professional golfer? How many tournaments does she play? What kind of preparation does she need to do? And what are professional golf tournaments like, anyway?

Keep in mind that Michelle has been playing alongside professionals since she was just twelve years old, when she became the youngest female to qualify for an LPGA event. She's known the pressure of performing at that level ever since. In 2003, she spent the entire summer doing nothing but traveling from tournament to tournament, logging more than twenty thousand miles in planes and rental cars. And that's what the life of a professional golfer generally consists of—travel. The PGA Tour holds forty-eight tournaments a year, the LPGA thirty-four. So most pros live out their lives during the season in hotel rooms and rented homes while they prepare for and play in one tournament after another.

But Michelle is still in high school and has no interest in adopting that lifestyle just yet. For now, she's content to play the occasional event—four to five events while school is in session, since she's not allowed to miss more than two weeks of school, twelve or thirteen total for the year. Because she isn't a member of the LPGA, she is only allowed to play in up to eight events—six under sponsor exemptions, plus the U.S. Women's Open and the Women's British Open, which aren't sponsored by the LPGA. Until she graduates from the Punahou School, she'll still be a relatively normal teenager—albeit one with an enormous fan following.

"Part of me wants to play every week," Michelle told the Associated Press. "But a big part of me wants to stay at school, be normal. That's very important to me and my family for me to go to school. I'm very grateful for that. If there were more days, I would love to play week after week after week, because that's what I love to do. But I love to go to school. That's a part of my life I can't live without right now." While most professional golfers spend their entire day practicing, Michelle has to squeeze it in after school. In class from 7:30 in the morning until 2:30 in the afternoon, she then heads over to the practice range to hit balls or play nine holes each day until 6:00. Four times a week she also heads to the gym to work out, then finally heads home for dinner.

In 2006, Michelle has already had a busy year. While juggling advanced precalculus, chemistry, and Japanese classes as a junior at Punahou, she's also played a tournament each month—in January it was the PGA Tour's Sony Open; in February, the LPGA's Fields Open; in March, the Kraft Nabisco Championship.

Playing only occasionally has its drawbacks, however. While regular professionals gain momentum by playing week to week, Michelle goes a month or more between tournaments. "That's the hardest part for me. I play one tournament; then I take a month off," she told the press before the Sony Open.

FAST FACT

Michelle's favorite subject? Chemistry. "You get to blow stuff up," she says.

"You can't just turn it off and turn it on," her coach, David Leadbetter, added. "We're never going to see what she's really capable of until she plays a bunch of tournaments in a row—on different courses with different conditions—on a regular basis. That's tough, even when she's hitting it well. The momentum factor isn't there. That's going to be an issue until she finishes school. It's tough to play twelve tournaments a year and really get your game firing on all cylinders."

And it's not just school and golf tournaments Michelle must juggle. With her endorsement contracts for Sony and Nike, Michelle has professional spokesperson duties as well. For Sony, she has shot a video and done some photo shoots. For Nike, she posed for their calendar and met with their designer to choose her clothes for the entire 2007 season. She gives numerous interviews to the press, from *Golf Digest* to *The Honolulu Advertiser,* to a Korean newspaper, the *Donga Ilbo,* where she confessed her love for Korean soap operas.

She's found that living a double life—that of a high school student and a professional golfer—has been a challenge but not impossible. "It hasn't been that hard to juggle stuff," she told the press. "I'm very grateful that Sony and Nike have been very understanding with my schedule. They understand that I'm just a kid and I go to school full-time."

THE 2006 SONY OPEN

Michelle began her third run at the Sony Open with high expectations. It was her fourth attempt on the PGA Tour, after all, and she had made her first LPGA cut on her fourth try—at the Kraft Nabisco Championship in 2003. Perhaps four would be her lucky number on the PGA Tour as well.

She practiced hard to prepare, playing three rounds a week at the Waialea Country Club—for free, thanks to the club owners. She came in knowing as much or more about the course as any pro there.

But day 1 did not go as planned. The wind was swirling, with gusts up to 40 miles an hour, and she found, as golfers often do in windy conditions, that she couldn't control her ball.

She opened with two pars, using her Nike SasQuatch driver to knock her first drive right past those of her playing partners. But then, on her third hole, she missed a 30-inch par putt to take a bogey and followed it up with a double bogey on the next. On the eighth hole she overshot the green and almost beaned her agent, Ross Berlin. Three double bogeys and four bogeys later, she signed her scorecard for a 9-over-par 79, the highest score she had shot to date on the PGA Tour.

Afterward, she told the press she couldn't believe she had played so poorly. "It was just a combination of bad shots that turned out to be really bad, and just a lot of wasted strokes out there," she said. "It was not my day."

Making the cut was looking less likely, if not impossible—she would have to shoot a 61 to be in the hunt. While that didn't happen, Friday did prove to be a vast improvement over the previous day—she shot seven birdies to come in at 68, tying her own record as a female playing against men.

"I was very crushed yesterday about how bad I played," Michelle told the press afterward. "But I woke up this morning and I just tried to relax out there and just tried to have fun out there and was trying to make a lot of birdies. I think I achieved that."

THE FIELDS OPEN

Her first event on the LPGA Tour in 2006 was the Fields Open, a first-time tournament that was played at her home course, Ko Olina on Oahu. Let's take a close look there to see what a typical LPGA tournament is like for Michelle.

First, it's important to understand the schedule for a professional tournament. While most LPGA tournaments last three or four days, from Thursday to either Saturday or Sunday, players generally arrive early to begin practicing, usually on the Monday or Tuesday before the tournament begins. Tues-

What's a Pro-Am?

A pro-am is a tournament within a tournament. The day before the real tournament begins, professionals who are playing in the tournament are teamed with four amateurs for one round of golf. The teams then compete with one another, using a captain's choice format (where the whole team plays from the position of the best ball). At the end of the day, prizes are given out to the best teams, the pros get in an extra practice round, and everyone has a great time.

Before you start thinking, "Hey, I want to be one of those amateurs," realize that it usually takes big bucks to get to play in a pro-am. The amateur competitors generally either are associated with the corporate sponsors of the event or pay a lot of money, thousands of dollars, for the privilege of playing with the pros. The money goes toward whatever charity the tournament supports, so it's all good.

Why a charity? Keep in mind that the LPGA is actually a nonprofit organization. Its primary purpose, other than to entertain the public with great golf shots, is to raise money for various causes. Each tournament supports a different cause. The Fields Open, for example, raised money for the Friends of Hawaii Charities, a group that in turn supports 250 nonprofit organizations in Hawaii.

days are reserved for practice rounds. Wednesday, the Tour members play in a pro-am (see the following sidebar).

Michelle isn't a member of the LPGA Tour (yet), so she doesn't have pro-am responsibilities, but for the Fields Open she arrived at the course on both Tuesday and Wednesday to play a practice round, hit balls on the range, practice putting, and do interviews.

Because Michelle is so popular, every member of the media (and there are always dozens, if not hundreds, of media members present for tournaments Michelle plays in) wants to ask her questions. She has multiple press conferences, as well as individual interviews—with the Golf Channel, with Japanese television, with ESPN and *Sports Illustrated,* and with newspapers worldwide. In every tournament she plays, she becomes the main story.

As Laura Neal, director of public relations for the LPGA, puts it, "Whenever Michelle Wie tees it up, more media follow her, more people tune in to our telecast, and more people get on the Web site and check out the scores." According to Neal, this helps the LPGA: "Maybe they haven't been interested in the past, but they're coming to check out Michelle Wie and they're staying because of all the personalities that we have to offer."

THE ROLEX WOMEN'S WORLD GOLF RANKINGS

Michelle gets asked all kinds of questions at tournament press conferences, from "What do you think of the course conditions today?" to "What is your relationship with Paula Creamer and Morgan Pressel?" She has to be quick on her feet, coming up with answers that will satisfy the media.

At the Fields Open, another question came up frequently: "What do you think of the World Golf Rankings?"

Just days before, the LPGA had announced a new system that would rank all of the female professional golfers in the world, regardless of which tour they played on or how much money they'd earned. It was called the Rolex Women's World Golf Rankings, and when it was unveiled for the first time, Michelle Wie appeared on the list in third place.

It was a surprise for everyone, including Michelle, that she placed so high on the list. After all, as a part-time golfer, she had barely played the minimum number of events—fifteen—to appear on the list at all. And to take the number-three spot in the world was quite a thrill. Annika Sorenstam took the top spot, Paula Creamer the second, and Michelle the third.

Many players who had won multiple LPGA tournaments appeared lower on the list than Michelle and thought it was unfair and inaccurate that Michelle, who had never won a professional tournament and had played in fewer than half of them, would land so high on the list.

So how did she end up third? Part of the way the rankings worked was that the fewer events a player had, the more each one was weighted. And majors counted for double the number of points of any other tournament. So Michelle, with fifteen events including six top tens and three top fives in majors, placed very high.

She was, of course, pleased with her position on the list—she hadn't expected to appear on it at all, let alone in third place. "I can't believe I was on the World Rankings," she told the press. "It was a cool feeling to be number three in the world. This is awesome. I can't believe it."

How did she feel about the negative reaction she was getting from the other players? "It's not like I put myself in number three," she pointed out. "All I did was play golf."

DURING TOURNAMENT WEEK, she's right—all she does is play golf. She plays multiple practice rounds and hits balls on the range and putts on the putting green for hours before the tournament even begins. After each round, she would head straight back to the practice range and hit balls long after it became too dark to see where the balls landed. With her parents and caddie, Greg Johnston, nearby, she would run putting drills again and again. And did it pay off?

The first two days of the Fields Open, she played well but not great. She went into the third and final round on Saturday at seven under—tied for ninth place. Interestingly enough, rival Morgan Pressel shot the same scores, 67-70, so when the two girls began their final round, they found themselves paired together.

This made for a great story—two young rivals touted as the future of women's golf paired together on the final round. Now everyone would see how their games matched up to each other. And while their scores on days 1 and 2 of the tournament were identical, day 3 was a different story. Michelle ended up shooting an impressive 66, beating out Morgan by five strokes.

As she began the par-4 eighteenth hole, Michelle was in great position—she had a share of the lead. After a solid 250-yard drive with her 3 wood, she knocked her second shot on the green about 8 feet from the flag. With a birdie here, she would own the lead outright. The putt, however, instead of breaking the way she thought it would, took a slight turn left and stayed outside the hole. She tapped in for her par, but now would begin the waiting game. The two ladies she was sharing the lead with, Seon-Hwa Lee and Meena Lee, were playing behind Michelle. If they made birdies, Michelle would be out of luck. With pars, Michelle would end up in a play-off, and if they made bogeys, the title would be hers, her first LPGA win.

But it wasn't meant to happen at the Fields Open. As it turned out, both of the Korean ladies made birdies, putting them in a play-off together, with Michelle in third place.

Still, she couldn't complain. She had been right there in contention, with a share of the lead when it counted most, and kept her nerves steady. At the end, she was beaten by her opponents, not by mistakes on her part. The only real mistake she made during the entire final round was a bogey on the par-5 thirteenth hole. For Michelle, a par 5 is normally a birdie opportunity. Because she is so long off the tee, she can usually put it on the green in just two shots, whereas it takes most women three. Then, even without a one-putt, she has a great chance to make a birdie.

But today the thirteenth gave her some problems. It took her the requisite three shots to get on the green because of a slightly errant drive into the rough. Still, she should have gotten down in two putts from the 20 feet she had left. Instead, she made a costly three-putt, leading to her only bogey of the round. Still, she had started the day with few people giving her a chance to win. And she came out with seven birdies to prove them wrong. She was right there in contention until the last shots were played.

After she putted out on the eighteenth, she was ushered into the scorer's tent to sign her card. Then, a long line of fans greeted her, asking for autographs—old men right alongside little girls. Finally, after a postround press conference, she was able to head for home—still not sure who had actually won the tournament, since Meena and Seon-Hwa Lee were still out on the course, in a three-hole play-off that Meena would eventually win.

So Michelle began the weekend ranked as the third-best female golfer in the world and ended the weekend in third place at the tournament. It was a fitting finish for her first 2006 LPGA outing. And it came with something else: a check for $73,227—her very first professional golf earnings.

Golf Tournaments: Things to Know
Before You Go

So you want to attend a professional golf tournament? Good idea—golf tournaments are as much fun to watch as they are to play. But before you arrive at the gates, there are a few things you should know.

First, you need to decide what kind of ticket you want to purchase. Golf tournaments generally offer two types—day passes and week passes. Day passes allow you entry for one day only. Week passes allow you entry all week—you can attend practice rounds, the pro-am, and each day of the tournament itself. Week passes offer the best value, and you have a much better chance of getting autographs and photos of your favorite players on practice-round days, rather than tournament days. On pretournament days, you'll find the atmosphere to be very relaxed, whereas on tournament days, players are very focused and serious and cameras are not allowed.

Second, you need to decide whether you want to walk the course with your favorite players or find a seat in the grandstand and watch players come through. Either way is equally fun, but be warned: If you choose to walk the course, wear comfortable shoes—walking an entire golf course is the equivalent of walking 5 miles! If you go the grandstand route, pick a seat where you can keep an eye on a leaderboard so you know what's happening. And make sure you keep a pairings sheet at hand, so you know who's coming through and when.

Finally, be aware that tournament spectators must follow golf etiquette, just like players do. Golf tournaments aren't like basketball or football games, where fans are encouraged to be as loud as possible. Instead, spectators must stay quiet most of the time. Only after the shot is completed do fans get to cheer. Normally you'll hear polite clapping for pars, with loud cheers reserved for birdies and eagles. Never, ever make any noise while a player is hitting or putting—not even a whisper—or you'll get an entire crowd giving you dirty looks, and you might even get a warning from a marshal.

14

The Next Step

**I don't want to follow in anyone's
footsteps. I want to make my own.**

So what's next for Michelle? Where will she go from here? At
just sixteen years old, she still must wait before she's eligible to
join the LPGA, not to mention before she graduates from high
school. For now, she faces some big decisions. And the outcome of those decisions is one of the most compelling stories
in golf.

Will she go on to college? Will she join the LPGA when she
turns eighteen? Will she earn her PGA Tour card? Will she
achieve her goal of playing in the Masters? This is a girl for
whom limitations don't seem to exist. Whatever happens,
Michelle Wie fans will enjoy watching her go for it.

The Golf Channel's Mark Rolfing asked her many of these
questions in a recent interview. She explained that her plan for
now is to graduate not only from the Punahou School but from
Stanford University as well. And while she loves Hawaii, she
realizes that a career in golf will probably require her to move
to the mainland before too long.

Michelle has made it clear that her goal is twofold: to play full-time on the LPGA in 2008 after she turns eighteen and to play on the PGA Tour as well, as soon as she can make it. Her old coach Casey Nakama says that he would like to see her join the PGA Tour, but that she should earn her spot the same way all its current members have—through qualifying.

"In fairness to the players, if she wants to play on the PGA Tour, she should go through the Tour Qualifying School," says Nakama. "If she did earn her way in that way, they're going to welcome her because they'll really respect her as a player. Right now, at this time, the players don't respect her as a player because she's getting all these exemptions. They're saying she's not earning her way into the tournaments by what she's accomplished; she's earning her way into the tournaments by the carnival, by people wanting to see how far she hits the ball. But based on her record, she's not worthy of the exemptions she's getting. That's why the players don't have respect for her. Not yet."

Tiger Woods faced some of the same issues when he first turned pro. Not having yet proved himself on Tour, he was offered millions in endorsements. But within a year he had won two tournaments, and within two years he was the number-one player. Michelle will need to prove herself through her play in the same way.

Whether she'll have to go through the LPGA's Qualifying School remains to be seen; there are, after all, other ways to join the Tour. One way is through Q-School, the multisectional annual tournament—that's how most members earn their cards. Another is by playing into the top-five spots on the Futures Tour, the LPGA's developmental tour. And a final way to earn a spot is by placing high on the LPGA's money list. The top ninety money earners on the LPGA Tour each year are automatically given membership for the next year. Place below 125th, and you lose your card. If Michelle, in the eight LPGA events she plays each year as a nonmember, earns enough to place in the top ninety of the LPGA's money list, she'll earn her card automatically. In 2005, her earnings, had she been a professional, would have topped $680,000—putting her sixteenth on the money list. Making it to the top ninety shouldn't be too difficult.

But is joining the LPGA really something she wants to do?

Carolyn Bivens, commissioner of the LPGA Tour, acknowledges that Michelle's two goals, playing on both tours, may conflict in some ways. If Michelle were to become a full-time member of the LPGA, then she would have to play in at least ten LPGA events—she would only be allowed two exceptions in order to play in a competing event. But many LPGA and PGA Tour events occur on the same weekend and would therefore compete with one another. This might cause problems down the road.

But Michelle may well find her own solution. As Bivens told the press, "Because there are other women and pioneers who have come before Michelle, she has the opportunity to do things differently. And the fact that doors are open to women to pursue different routes is always a good thing. . . . She represents not the norm. She has kind of done it her own way. She represents some of the very best young talent. I even think the way she has chosen to do it, which is a little bit nontraditional, kind of matches the whole iconoclastic personality."

Meanwhile, Michelle wants to have as normal a life as possible. She enjoys the same things that most kids her age enjoy—spending time with friends, hanging out at the mall, going to movies. On the big stage, yes, life has changed quite a bit for her since she turned pro. On the smaller one, her life at school, it hasn't changed much at all.

For now, she plans to keep it that way. She still wants to go to college, and along with her favorite little teddy bear, Sam, she keeps a little stuffed cow on her golf bag—a cow that wears a "Stanford" T-shirt. She's been successful at both golf and academics so far, with her hybrid approach; there's no reason to think she can't continue as she gets older.

Michelle's family will probably leave Hawaii after Michelle finishes high school. For now, they want to stay so that she can graduate from the Punahou School. But after graduating, she'll be able to play professional golf full-time, and that will require living where the golf is—on the mainland.

The Wies have already purchased a home at Bighorn Golf Club, in Palm Desert, California. For the moment they're using it as a base of operations for training and tournaments—the Samsung World Championship is played there, and Mission Hills, where the Kraft Nabisco is played each year, is only fifteen minutes away. Another possible spot they might consider moving to is Florida. From there, Michelle would have access to her coach, David Leadbetter, and everyone who trains with him. Many professional golfers call Florida home.

ACCEPTING NO LIMITATIONS

After the Sony Open, Michelle was asked whether she pays attention when people criticize her choices, asking what she's trying to prove. And she said it best herself when she answered, "This is what I want to do and I think that what I want to do is most important. . . . My goal is definitely to win in the

LPGA, win a major. My goal is definitely to make the cut and to compete [on the PGA Tour, too]. I don't think that there's actually real strict guidelines how to do it, and I think that what I'm doing might be right, might be wrong, but it's what I want to do right now and it makes me happy, so I intend to keep on doing it."

And as long as she keeps trying, she's already succeeding at another of her goals. Remember what she told her sports psychologist at their first meeting? That she considers herself to be on a mission, one that will communicate to women that there really are no boundaries.

Michelle's life in golf is communicating just that. With the combination that she embodies—talent along with hard work—there's no limit to what she might accomplish.

Michelle's Accomplishments Through the Years

2000

- Joined Oahu's Junior Golf Association at age ten. Won five of the seven tournaments she entered her first year.

- Qualified for the Women's Amateur Public Links Championship. Became the youngest to qualify for a USGA amateur tournament (age ten).

- Played in the Hawaii State Open, an event for adults; was the low amateur in the Women's Division.

- Won the Honolulu Mayor's Cup.

- Played in the Hawaii State Women's Stroke Play Championship; took third place.

2001

▸ Qualified again for the Women's Amateur Public Links Championship. Advanced to the third round of match play.

▸ Played in the Hawaii State Open, Women's Division. Took second place.

▸ Won the Hawaii State Junior Golf Association's Tournament of Champions.

▸ Won the Hawaii State Women's Stroke Play Championship (one of three major tournaments in Hawaii). Became the youngest winner, at age eleven.

▸ Won the prestigious Jennie K. Wilson Invitational, a tournament for amateur women, by nine strokes. Became the tournament's youngest-ever winner, at age eleven.

▸ Played against men for the first time in the ninety-third Manoa Cup Hawaii State Amateur Match-Play Championship, normally an all-male tournament in Honolulu. She became not only the youngest player to qualify, at age eleven, but also the first woman.

2002

▸ FEBRUARY: Qualified for her first LPGA event, the Take-fuji Classic. At twelve years old, she became the youngest woman ever to qualify for an LPGA event. Shot 72-74, missed the cut.

Became the youngest female ever to qualify for and play in the Hawaii Pearl Open.

▷ MARCH: Became the first female and the youngest player to make the cut at the Hawaii State Amateur Stroke-Play Championship. She ended up tied for seventeenth.

▷ MAY: Played in her second LPGA event, the Asahi Ryokuken International. Shot 81-75, missed the cut.

Played in the Hickam Invitational, a men's event in Hawaii. Tied for fifth place.

▷ JUNE: Qualified for and played in the ninety-fourth Manoa Cup Hawaii State Amateur Match-Play Championship, normally an all-male event. Became the youngest female to advance to the second round of match play.

Qualified for the U.S. Women's Amateur Public Links Championship. Became the youngest to advance to semi-finals, at age twelve.

▷ JULY: Youngest junior medalist at the Women's Trans National Amateur Championship.

Tied for seventh place at the Westfield Junior PGA Championship (one of junior golf's major championships).

Michelle's Accomplishments Through the Years

Qualified for the USGA Girl's Junior Championship, a
national tournament. Advanced to match play.

▷ AUGUST: Qualified and played in her third LPGA
event, the Wendy's Championship for Children. Shot 77-
75, missed the cut by two strokes.

Played in her second men's event of the year, the
Barber's Point Invitational in Hawaii. Tied for fourth
place.

▷ NOVEMBER: Played in the Hawaii State Open,
Women's Division. Blew the field away, winning by thirteen strokes.

▷ DECEMBER: Won the Hawaii State Junior Golf Association's Tournament of Champions for the second year in a
row.

2003

▷ JANUARY: Attempted to qualify for the PGA Tour's
Sony Open.

▷ FEBRUARY: Played in the Hawaii Pearl Open, where she
was the only female among male pros from the Japan
Tour, and became the youngest player and only female
ever to make the cut, at thirteen years old. She tied for
forty-third.

Michelle's Accomplishments Through the Years

▶ MARCH: Played in the Hawaii State Amateur Stroke-Play Championship, where she was one of only three females. She tied for fourth.

Played in the LPGA's Kraft Nabisco Championship, a major, making an LPGA cut for the first time. Shot 72-74-66-72 and tied for ninth. The 66 tied for the lowest score ever made by an amateur in a major.

▶ APRIL: Played in the LPGA's Chick-fil-A Charity Championship hosted by Nancy Lopez. Shot 72-70-71 to tie for thirty-third place.

▶ JUNE: Won her first national championship—the U.S. Women's Amateur Public Links Championship—and became the youngest winner in the 108-year history of the event.

Played in the LPGA's ShopRite Classic. Shot 71-72-72 to tie for fifty-second place.

▶ JULY: Played in the U.S. Women's Open. Shot 73-73-76-76 to tie for thirty-ninth place.

Played in the U.S. Girl's Junior Amateur Championship. Advanced to the third round of match play.

▶ AUGUST: Played in the U.S. Women's Amateur Championship. Qualified for match play.

Played in the LPGA's Jamie Farr Kroger Classic. Shot 73-72 and missed the cut.

Played in the Canadian Tour's Bay Mills Open Players Championship, a men's event. Shot 74-79 and missed the cut.

SEPTEMBER: Became the first female to play in a Nationwide Tour event, the Albertsons Boise Open. Shot 78-76 and missed the cut.

Played in the LPGA's Safeway Classic. Shot 69-72-73 to tie for twenty-eighth.

OCTOBER: Played in the LPGA's Nine Bridges Classic on Cheju Island, South Korea. Shot 85-78-70 to place sixty-ninth.

2004

JANUARY: Played in her first PGA Tour event, the Sony Open. Shot 72-68 (even par) and missed the cut by one stroke. At fourteen years old, she was both the youngest to play in a PGA Tour event and the first female to score in the sixties on the PGA Tour.

FEBRUARY: Played in the Hawaii Pearl Open against male professionals. Shot 2-under-par, which was the lowest score for a female amateur in the history of the tournament, and tied for thirty-eighth place.

MARCH: Played in the LPGA's Safeway International. Shot 72-67-70-77 and tied for nineteenth place.

Played in the Kraft Nabisco Championship, an LPGA major, for the second time. Shot 69-72-69-71 (7-under-par) and placed fourth.

▷ MAY: Played in the LPGA's Michelob Ultra Open. Shot 72-67-73-72 and tied for twelfth.

▷ JUNE: Became the youngest player ever to be selected to represent the United States for the Curtis Cup team. Won both of her singles matches and finished with a 2-2 record.

Runner-up (second place) at the U.S. Women's Amateur Public Links Championship.

Played in the U.S. Amateur Public Links sectional qualifier against men but failed to qualify.

▷ JULY: Played in the U.S. Women's Open, a major. Shot 71-70-71-73 (1-over-par) to tie for thirteenth place. Tied with Paula Creamer for low amateur honors.

Played in the Evian Masters. Shot 71-71-76-69 to take thirty-third place.

▷ AUGUST: Played in the U.S. Women's Amateur Championship. Advanced to the second round of match play.

Played in the LPGA's Wendy's Championship for Children. Shot 73-69-71-69 to tie for sixth place.

▷ SEPTEMBER: Played in the Waikoloa Open, a local event in Hawaii. Tied for second place in the amateur division.

▷ OCTOBER: Played in the LPGA's Samsung World
  Championship. Shot 74-72-67-70 (5-under-par) and tied
  for thirteenth place.

2005

▷ JANUARY: Played in her second PGA Tour event, the
  Sony Open. Shot 75-74 and missed the cut by seven
  strokes.

▷ FEBRUARY: Played in the LPGA's SBS Open. Shot 70-70-
  70 (6-under-par) and tied for second place, her best finish
  to date in an LPGA event.

▷ MARCH: Played in the LPGA's Safeway International.
  Shot 73-67-73-71 (4-under-par) and tied for twelfth place.

  Played in the Kraft Nabisco Championship, a major. Shot
  70-74-73-71 (even par) and tied for fourteenth place.

▷ JUNE: Played in the McDonald's LPGA Championship,
  a major. Shot 69-71-71-69 (8-under-par) to take second
  place, her best finish in an LPGA major.

  Played in the U.S. Women's Open, a major. Shot 69-73-
  72-82 to place twenty-third.

▷ JULY: Played in her third PGA Tour event, the John
  Deere Classic. Shot 70-71 (1-under-par) but missed the
  cut by two strokes.

Played in the seventy-seventh U.S. Amateur Public Links Championship (a men's USGA event). First beat eighty-three men to qualify, then won three matches to become the youngest player and first female to advance to the quarterfinals.

Played in the Evian Masters. Shot 75-70-68-68 (7-under-par) to tie for second place. Had she been a professional, she would have earned $212,283.

Played in the Weetabix Women's British Open, her fourth LPGA major of the year. Shot 75-67-67-69 to tie for third place.

▷ OCTOBER: Turned professional.

Played in the LPGA's Samsung World Championship. Shot 70-65-71-74 to finish fourth, only to be disqualified.

▷ NOVEMBER: Played in the Casio World Open, an event on the men's Japan Tour. Shot 73–75 and missed the cut by one stroke.

Glossary

Golf has a language all its own. Here are the meanings of some terms you might not have heard before.

AJGA: The American Junior Golf Association—a nonprofit organization dedicated to competitive golf for juniors (golfers aged twelve to eighteen). The AJGA holds seventy-five tournaments each year, all around the country. Anyone twelve to eighteen years old can join the AJGA, but entrance into tournaments has to be earned based on performance.

Amateur: According to the USGA, an amateur golfer is one "who plays the game as a non-remunerative and non-profit-making sport and who does not receive remuneration for teaching golf or for other activities because of golf skill or reputation, except as provided in the Rules." In plain English, an amateur is a person who doesn't get paid for playing golf. Most golfers are amateurs. If amateurs play in pro tournaments, they're not allowed to keep any money they

Glossary

might have won. Players are very careful about maintaining amateur status, because once a player switches from amateur to pro status, they can no longer play on a college team or accept a college golf scholarship.

Approach shot: The shot that takes a player from the fairway onto the green. It's called the "approach" shot because you're "approaching" the flag. An approach shot requires the most accuracy—you want to hit the ball as close to the flag as possible, to save yourself from having to make a long putt.

Birdie: Finishing a hole in one stroke less than par. Professional golfers usually make several birdies in a round. Mere mortals are usually pretty happy simply making par.

Bogey: Finishing a hole in one stroke more than par. Making a 5 on a par-4 hole, for example. Two strokes higher than par is called a double bogey.

Bunker: Also called sand traps, bunkers punish golfers for bad shots. When a ball goes into a bunker, it stops—basically the equivalent of putting on the brakes. That means a golfer will require more shots to complete the hole.

Chip shot: A very short shot, normally hit with a pitching wedge or short iron, that is hit lightly from just off the green, and then rolls to the flag.

Cut: In golf, the word "cut" has several meanings. The first meaning has to do with the length of the grass on a golf course. The "first cut" is the section of grass just off the fairway. The "second cut" is the rough—the long grass that's very hard to hit out of. Another meaning refers to the cut in a tournament. After the first two rounds of a golf tournament, the field (the group of competitors) is cut in half. If you're in the bottom 50 percent, you have "missed the cut," and you're out of the tournament. Only the top half of the field advances to the weekend rounds. The players who make the cut get to divide the prize money among themselves— the higher you place on the leaderboard, the more money you make, with the winner making the most, of course. Miss the cut, and you make no money at all. The word "cut" can also refer to the direction a golf ball travels in the air— if it moves left to right, it's called a slice or cut.

Divot: The hole that's left in the fairway when a golfer hits the ball and takes a chunk of grass and dirt with it.

Draw: A golf shot where the ball starts off going straight and then curves slightly to the left (the opposite of a fade). Very good golfers do this deliberately to shape their ball to the hole.

Driver: The biggest golf club—it hits the ball the farthest but is also the most difficult to control and can therefore get players into trouble.

Eagle: Finishing a hole in two strokes less than par. Making a hole-in-one on a par 3, for example, or a 3 on a par 5. Eagles are very rare and very thrilling.

Fade: A golf shot where the ball starts off going straight and then curves slightly to the right (the opposite of a draw). Very good golfers do this deliberately to shape their ball to the hole.

Fairway: The wide path of short grass that runs from the tee box all the way up to the green. Grass is kept short and manicured in the fairway, which makes it easy to hit the ball. This rewards players for hitting good, straight tee shots.

Field: No, we're not talking about a piece of land. In golf, the word "field" refers to the group of people competing in a tournament. A 144-person field, for example, means the tournament has 144 people playing in it.

Futures Tour (officially, the Duramed FUTURES Tour): This is the LPGA's "developmental tour." If women aren't quite good enough to play on the LPGA Tour, they can try out for the Futures Tour and gain valuable professional competitive experience. The Futures Tour holds eighteen to twenty tournaments annually, and at the end of the year the top five money winners gain their LPGA card. Many current LPGA members once played on the Futures Tour.

Gallery: The crowd of spectators watching a golf tournament.

Green: The very well-manicured area of grass around the hole. The grass is kept extremely short there so that the ball will roll easily and quickly.

Grip: The way a player holds the club in their hands. The grip plays a large role in the direction the ball travels. Grips are described as strong, weak, or neutral.

Handicap: Handicaps were created so people with different skill levels can compete with one another. The formula for figuring a handicap is very complicated, but basically, a person's handicap is the number of strokes between their average score and par. If they generally score about ten strokes over par, their handicap will be around a 10. The lower the handicap, the better the golfer. Professional golfers have no handicap at all, whereas the average recreational golfer can have a handicap anywhere from 10 to 30 or even higher.

Honors: Whoever scores best on a hole gets to tee off first on the next hole. That person is said to have "the honors."

Hook: A bad golf shot where the ball moves from right to left, an extreme version of a draw (opposite of a slice).

Irons: Golf clubs with smallish, wedge-shaped heads. They're used when a player needs to be very accurate, such as on approach shots. The other type of golf club is called a wood— these have large, rounded heads and are used for hitting the ball a greater distance. Irons are numbered 1 to 9, plus the wedges (sand wedge, pitching wedge, and lob wedge).

Junior: Golfers eighteen and under are considered "juniors." Many tournaments are open only to juniors, so kids can play in events with people their own age.

Leaderboard: The giant scoreboard at golf tournaments that lists the top players in a tournament. The better you do, the higher on the leaderboard you are.

Lie: The way a ball is resting in the grass is called its lie. Having a *good lie* means your ball came to rest in a favorable position—it will be easy to hit. Having a *bad lie* means that the ball will be difficult to hit—perhaps it stopped next to a tree, under a bush, or in a divot.

Line: On the green, the invisible line between a player's ball and the hole. Whatever you do, don't step in anyone's line! You might muss that delicate grass, which could affect their putt.

LPGA: Ladies Professional Golf Association.

Match play: This is the method of scoring whereby the winner is the player who wins the most holes, rather than the person who has the lowest overall score. It's different from *stroke play,* whereby the winner is the person with the lowest score after eighteen holes.

Medalist honors: Sometimes big tournaments have "qualifiers" to determine who's allowed to join the field. The winner of the qualifier is given "medalist honors"—they didn't win the tournament, but they did place first in the qualifier.

Nationwide Tour: This is the PGA's "developmental tour," similar to the Futures Tour for the LPGA. If players aren't quite good enough to join the PGA Tour, they can try out for the Nationwide Tour and gain valuable professional competitive experience. In 2006, the Nationwide Tour will hold thirty-one tournaments, and at the end of the year the top twenty-one money winners will gain their PGA Tour cards. Many current PGA Tour members once played on the Nationwide Tour.

Par: The number of strokes it should take a good player to complete a hole. The ideal hole should be played with two putts, plus whatever the required number it takes to get to the green. For example, a good player should play a par-5 hole in five strokes: three to reach the green, plus two putts. The same player should reach a par 3 in one shot, then take two putts to complete the hole in three strokes. A golf course has a par, too. Most courses are par 72s.

Pin (or flagstick): The pole that sticks out of the hole so that golfers can see the hole from a distance. The flag on the end of the pole makes it more visible and also tells golfers which way the wind is blowing.

Pitch shot: A short, high golf shot, usually hit with a pitching wedge or sand wedge.

Range: A practice area where golfers can hit buckets of balls at various targets. Professional golfers spend many, many hours on the range perfecting their swing.

Rough: The long grass outside of the fairway. It is deliberately left long to make it more difficult to hit out of, thereby penalizing a player for an imperfect shot.

Scratch: A player who is so good, they don't have a handicap. That is, they usually shoot par.

Slice: A bad golf shot where the ball moves from left to right, an extreme version of a fade. Also called a *cut*.

Stroke: Any time your club hits the ball, it's considered a "stroke" and is added to your score. A 300-yard drive is a stroke, and a 2-inch putt is also a stroke.

Glossary

Stroke play: Also called *medal play,* this is the method of scoring whereby the winner is the person who has the lowest overall score at the end of eighteen holes. It differs from *match play,* which is played hole by hole, with the winner being the person who wins the most holes.

Tee: The little plastic or wooden T-shaped device on which golfers place their ball before hitting. You can only use a tee at the beginning of a hole, on a tee box.

Tee box: The small, flat patch of grass that golfers stand in when beginning a golf hole. You'll always find two *tee markers* on the tee box, showing the golfer where to stand and place the ball.

Tee time: Literally, the time a player begins their round of golf. In a golf tournament, tee times during the first two days are determined by a random draw. On days three and four, tee times are determined by a player's position on the leaderboard, with the best players teeing off last.

USGA: United States Golf Association. It exists to promote the game of golf, and it does so by holding thirteen tournaments each year, for both amateurs and professionals. It also regulates the game of golf, by underwriting the rules here in the United States.

Wedge: A type of iron used for short distances or trouble shots, such as hitting out of sand.

Wood: The largest type of golf club, with a big, rounded clubhead. Once upon a time they were made out of actual wood, hence the name. But these days, they're usually made out of high-tech metals. Woods hit the ball farther than irons do, but they're somewhat less accurate. Players hit woods from tee boxes, to start off a hole, or from the fairway if they have a long way to the hole.

Resources

American Junior Golf Association (AJGA)
1980 Sports Club Drive
Braselton, GA 30517
Phone: (770) 868-4200
Fax: (770) 868-4211
www.ajga.org

The David Leadbetter Golf Academy
5500 34th Street West
Bradenton, FL 34210
Phone: (941) 755-1000
Fax: (941) 752-2531
www.imgacademies.com

Ladies Professional Golf Association (LPGA)
100 International Golf Drive
Daytona Beach, FL 32124-1092
Phone: (386) 274-6200

Fax: (386) 274-1099
www.lpga.com

Olomana Golf Links

Casey Nakama Golf Development Center
41-1801 Kalanianaole Highway
Waimanalo, HI 96795
Phone: (808) 259-7712
www.olomanagolflinks.com

PGA of America

100 Avenue of the Champions
Palm Beach Gardens, FL 33418
Phone: (407) 624-8400
Fax: (407) 624-8448
www.pga.com/home

PGA Tour

112 TPC Boulevard
Ponte Verde, FL 32082
Phone: (904) 285-3700
Fax: (904) 285-7913
www.pgatour.com

United States Golf Association (USGA)

P.O. Box 708
Far Hills, NJ 07931
Phone: (908) 234-2300
Fax: (908) 234-9687
www.usga.org